Copyright© 2006 by Landauer Corporation

Projects Copyright© 2006 by Lynette Jensen

This book was designed, produced, and published by Landauer Books
A division of Landauer Corporation
3100 NW 101st Street, Urbandale, Iowa 50322
www.landauercorp.com

President: Jeramy Lanigan Landauer
Editor-in-Chief: Becky Johnston
Art Director: Laurel Albright
Creative Director: Lynette Jensen
Photographers: Craig Anderson and Dennis Kennedy
Photostyling: Lynette Jensen and Margaret Sindelar
Technical Writer: Sue Bahr
Technical Illustrators: Lisa Kirchoff and Linda Bender

We also wish to thank the support staff of the Thimbleberries® Design Studio:
Sherry Husske, Virginia Brodd, Renae Ashwill, Ardelle Paulson, Kathy Lobeck, Carla Plowman,
Julie Jergens, Pearl Baysinger, Tracy Schrantz, Amy Albrecht, Leone Rusch, and Julie Borg.

The following manufacturers are licensed to sell Thimbleberries® products:
Thimbleberries® Rugs (www.colonialmills.com);
Thimbleberries® Quilt Stencils (www.quiltingcreations.com); and
Thimbleberries® Sewing Thread (www.robison-anton.com).

This book is printed on acid-free paper.

Printed in China 10 9 8 7 6 5 4 3 2 1

Library of Congress Cataloging-in-Publication Data

Jensen, Lynette.
    Thimbleberries new collection of classic quilts / by Lynette Jensen.
      p.cm.
    ISBN 1-890621-98-6
    1. Quilting--Patterns. 2. Patchwork--Patterns. 3. Appliqué--Patterns.
      I. Title: New collection of classic quilts. II. Thimbleberries, Inc. III. Title.

TT835.J5 2006
746.46'041--dc22   2005055251

                                                        ISBN 10: 1-890621-98-6
                                                        ISBN 13: 978-1-890621-98-8

THIMBLEBERRIES®

New Collection of
Classic Quilts

by Lynette Jensen

LANDAUER BOOKS

Table of
CONTENTS

FOREWORD

From my earliest childhood through 38 years of marriage to Neil, my fondest memories are of time spent with family and friends at "the cabin." In the early 1950s my parents and an aunt and uncle bought a lot on Lake Minnie Belle near the town where we lived in Minnesota. Together they built a small two-bedroom cabin with a fantastic view of the spring-fed lake—40-feet deep with cold, clear water. In those days, central air conditioning was at best a remote possibility for most. During the hot summer months, we eagerly awaited Dad's return from work so we could go for an evening dip in the lake. On these day trips, my sister Jan, myself, and our cousin Evy stayed in the water until our "bones got cold" and often were treated to a 5-cent ice cream cone on the way home. This relaxing respite from the summer heat made for a blissful bedtime in homes without air conditioning.

Since the cabin was built mostly on weekends, it was under construction for most of a summer, always on the "budget plan." The fireplace wall was built from bricks salvaged from an old schoolhouse and the walls were fashioned from cardboard boxes used for shipping mattresses. I recall

The cabin as it is today— a welcoming retreat for the third as well as future generations of our family.

many summer days spent chipping the old mortar from the weathered bricks. By the time we were finished, there were enough usable bricks to build a fireplace for the neighbor's cabin as well. As you can see from the photos below, my mother Lauretta used the fireplace for popping corn and my father Clayton, used it as a backdrop for showcasing his prized fishing catch—a Northern Pike. The original knotty pine kitchen cupboards which remain to this day have been lightened by "pickling," with sturdy pine walls added to match in 1989. As our son, Matt, noted it was more of a "model" than a remodel. The cabin was an integral part of my courtship and marriage to Neil, whose family also had a cabin across the lake. We're shown below with our son Matthew and our daughter, Kerry, who loved to spend summer afternoons daydreaming in the rowboat.

In 1999, we made a final change to the cabin by bumping out the living room wall to add a three-season porch that offers a more expansive view of the lake and the surrounding landscape of trees and shoreline. Even the garage in back of the cabin reflects the spirit of lake country, sporting a fish weather vane shown opposite in the last light of a long summer day.

Just as much of my childhood was spent at the cabin enjoying the water and fishing off the dock, so was that of our children. Matt and Kerry are shown here lounging in their inner tubes and in the boat fishing with Grandpa. And, one of my favorite photos is that of Matt and Neil catching the summer breeze in our small sailboat. During their teen and college years, it was a favorite gathering spot for our kids and their "dock jock" friends who were eager to help put the dock out in late spring and use the powerboat for fishing and waterskiing. Now grownup and busy with careers, Matt and Kerry along with her husband Trevor still look forward to weekends at the cabin.

Because some of my happiest memories are of the rest and relaxation offered by the cabin, it is not surprising that many of the quilts I've designed over the years reflect that same sense of calm and comfort in their patterns and color combinations. On the following pages, I've gathered up 26 of my favorites along with several pillows and optional colorways for a new collection of classic quilts that I hope will bring you as much pleasure and comfort as they have to my family and friends.

My best,

Lynette Jensen

A fairly recent addition to the cabin, the porch offers a relaxing view of the lake and a quiet corner for reading, resting or playing board games.

A restful retreat…
by the shore

INTRODUCTION

Discover how easy it is to make anywhere you live a welcome escape. Whether your home is in the city or the country and you can only dream of a cabin in the woods or a cottage by the sea, experience the joys of weekends all the time with quilts designed by Lynette Jensen for Thimbleberries®. Take time out to relax, renew and refuel in a retreat you can create in no time at all with a collection of classic quilts that range from small to generous.

On the following pages, choose from quilts with classic Thimbleberries® character, color and continuity that range in size to serve as seasonal accents for small-space decorating, cozy medium-sized throws for couches and chairs, and comfortable sleeping beauties for bedtime bliss. By surrounding yourself with quilts that transcend seasons and style, you'll find it easy to make weekends a way of life.

A restful retreat…
by the fireplace

Warm up any room with a fireplace as the focal point. Fuel the fires of your imagination by gathering up favorite "finds" that set the scene. Here, the nautical theme is carried around the room with well-worn oars, nets, framed photos of boats, sandpails and a mantel topped with a miniature sailboat replica.

For color and contrast, combine bright red and blue with splashes of white and sage to cool it all down a bit—as aptly demonstrated by the couch, rocker and old painted pine table which serves as a coffee table and nesting place for a pair of children's library chairs.

The quilt used as a cozy throw on the couch is an alternate colorway of the Block Party quilt featured on page 172. Plenty of accent pillows in coordinating colors complement the quilt, rustic furnishings, and the Thimbleberries® floor rug which ties it all together.

A restful retreat…
on the porch

Almost any corner can be transformed into a comfortable conversation area with soft comforts such as the throw pillows and an alternate colorway of the Hourglass Patches quilt featured on page 100. Creating a special summer hideaway often requires more imagination than money. Filling the cabin with an eclectic mix of old and new reflects Lynette's decorating style. For instance, Lynette counts the blue table in the foreground as one of the best garage-sale buys to date.

The stenciled pattern of simple quilt blocks adds fun color and design to a sturdy plank table built years ago by her Dad from the roof boards salvaged from Grandma Halverson's tiny farm house when it was being torn down.

A restful retreat...
in the bedroom

Curl up with your favorite look—in a bedroom brimming with northwoods nostalgia. Start with a generously-sized quilt for the bed like the alternate version shown here of the Holly Goose Chase quilt featured on page 196. Because the bedrooms in the cabin are quite casual, Lynette put found items to good use serving as decorative, yet practical accessories.

For example, the dresser shown above was already in distressed condition when Lynette received it from her mother. Stenciled pine cones and a large market basket overflowing with greens and berries provide almost instant rehab for a much-needed storage piece.

Likewise, the old wooden screen door trimmed with neat rows of branches becomes the backdrop for an unusual tabletop twig cabin—a classic piece of folk art built by creative hands in the past.

The large red trunk is an old family piece from her great grandmother. It traveled to the United States from Germany when Lynette's ancestors made their way to Minnesota.

Take time for tea in a nook sized just right for two. Spending a few minutes at the end of the day to unwind together can be as relaxing as a drive in the country. Find a space that is underutilized and surround yourself with a few decorative and personal touches that are meaningful to you. Lynette's mismatched pottery collection fills nooks and crannies with color and interest.

The unusual antique three-tiered corner shelf made of dozens of painted wooden spools, above, was made to stand alone, but Lynette put it to better use perched on a table top as part of a corner display. Another eclectic grouping of white and sage-colored ceramic pieces is enhanced by a pair of weather-worn shutters serving as a backdrop for a framed floral print.

A restful retreat…
on the patio

As the days grow longer and warmer, while away the weekends on the patio. Dress up the table with a mix of vintage linens and a cornucopia of garden blooms. Savor the sunset with good food and good friends for a relaxing evening at home. To create a personal and more private retreat, add a garden arbor to frame the view. Fill pots and wicker baskets with perennial reminders of your love for gardening.

A restful retreat…
in the garden

In search of serenity?

Look no further than your own backyard. All
you'll need for this journey are some basic tools,
a watering can and rustic seating. Experience the
joyful solitude of the weekend gardener when
you set aside your cares and concerns and just
"sit for a spell." Let nature's beauty be your
guide as you discover the simple sights and
sounds of summer—birds and butterflies on the
wing and bees buzzing busily in the background.

Put down roots indoors and outdoors for the best of both worlds. Building your dream house couldn't be easier—just fill the backyard with a collection of miniature houses and birdhouses to add interest to the garden. Whether you're relaxing or working in the yard, these little treasures bring joy to the day.

To better display vintage houses and pails full of perennials, add a lower-cost accent table by turning two urn-style planters upside down with a distressed shutter as the tabletop. This table works well as a base for spring, summer, autumn and winter seasonal arrangements.

PREVIEW

Back by popular demand, Lynette Jensen has gathered 28 of her best-selling Thimbleberries® designs into a new collection of classic quilts featured on the following pages in three distinct groupings. Ranging in size from small to medium to large, many of the pieced quilts and throws are accented with easy appliqué which will appeal to a wide audience of quilters.

The quilts, throws and pillows are grouped by size into three chapters: Weekend Wonders, Casual Comforts, and Bedtime Bliss. Each chapter includes enduring quilt patterns using the extensive Thimbleberries® fabric collections designed for RJR fabrics.

Several of the featured quilts are also offered in alternate colorways. Discover for yourself how the changing of color combinations creates a dramatically different look—and take on the challenge by experimenting with fabric combinations of your choosing.

Whether you're a beginner, intermediate, or even a master quilter, you'll find a Thimbleberries® quilt well worth the time and investment it takes to make a keepsake quilt that will pass from generation to generation.

Weekend WONDERS

Little quilts, displayed as wall hangings, table toppers and runners, set the mood for almost any room's seasonal decorating. On the following pages choose from themes ranging from harvest to holiday that blend perfectly to transition you through the year in style.

A Garden House

A birdhouse bordered with
blossoms is the perfect wall decor for
cottage or cabin. To complement an
indoor display, simply surround a vintage
birdhouse with buckets of blooms.

A Garden House

36 x 40-inches

Fabrics & Supplies

1/2 yard **BROWN PRINT**
for roof and house sections

3/4 yard **RED PRINT**
for birdhouse and outer border

1/2 yard **BEIGE PRINT #1**
for birdhouse background

3/8 yard **BLACK PRINT**
for inner border and birdhouse holes

3/8 yard **GREEN PRINT #1**
for narrow middle border

3/4 yard **BEIGE PRINT #2**
for wide middle border

3/4 yard **GREEN PRINT #2**
for vine and oak leaf appliqués

1/8 yard **GREEN PRINT #3** for small leaf appliqués

1/8 yard **BLUE PRINT** for flower appliqués

1/8 yard **GOLD PRINT** for flower center appliqués

1/8 yard **ROSE PRINT** for berry appliqués

1/2 yard **GREEN PRINT #1** for binding

1-3/8 yards backing fabric

quilt batting, at least 42 x 46-inches

paper-backed fusible web

template material

machine embroidery thread or pearl cotton:
black, gold

tear-away fabric stabilizer (optional)

Before beginning this project,
read through **Getting Started** on page 210.

Birdhouse Block

Cutting

From **BROWN PRINT:**
• Cut 1, 6-7/8-inch square
• Cut 3, 2 x 15-1/2-inch rectangles

From **RED PRINT:**
• Cut 2, 5 x 12-1/2-inch rectangles
• Cut 2, 3-1/2-inch squares

From **BEIGE PRINT #1:**
• Cut 1, 6-7/8-inch square
• Cut 2, 2 x 42-inch strip. From the strips cut:
    2, 2 x 6-1/2-inch rectangles
    4, 2 x 5-inch rectangles
    6, 2-inch squares

Piecing

Step 1   With right sides together, layer the
6-7/8-inch **BEIGE #1** and **BROWN** squares.
Press together, but do not sew. Cut the layered
square in half diagonally to make 2 sets of triangles.
Stitch 1/4-inch from the diagonal edge of each pair
of triangles; press.

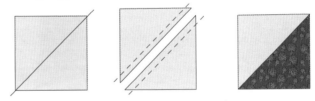

Make 2, 6-1/2-inch triangle-pieced squares

Step 2   With right sides together, position a
3-1/2-inch **RED** square on the **BROWN** corner of
each triangle-pieced square. Draw a diagonal line on
the **RED** square; stitch on the line. Trim the seam
allowance to 1/4-inch; press.

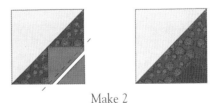

Make 2

Step 3   Sew the triangle-pieced square units
together; press. Sew the 2 x 6-1/2-inch **BEIGE #1**
rectangles to both side edges of the unit; press.

<u>At this point the roof unit should measure 6-1/2 x 15-1/2-inches.</u>

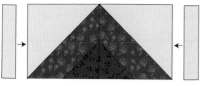

Make 1

Step 4 With right sides together, position 2-inch **BEIGE #1** squares on both corners of a 2 x 15-1/2-inch **BROWN** rectangle. Draw a diagonal line on the squares; stitch, trim, and press.

Make 3

Step 5 To add the Birdhouse Holes to the 5 x 12-1/2-inch **RED** rectangles, refer to **Appliqué - Fusible Web Method** on page 34.

Step 6 Sew a 2 x 5-inch **BEIGE #1** rectangle to both side edges of the 5 x 12-1/2-inch **RED** rectangles; press. <u>At this point each unit should measure 5 x 15-1/2-inches.</u>

Make 2

Step 7 Referring to the block diagram for placement, sew the birdhouse sections together; press. <u>At this point the birdhouse block should measure 15-1/2 x 20-inches.</u>

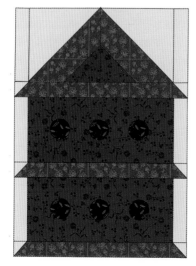

Borders

Note: *The yardage given allows for the border strips to be cut on the crosswise grain. Diagonally piece the strips as needed, referring to* **Diagonal Piecing** *instructions on page 215. Read through* **Border** *instructions on page 214 for general instructions on adding borders.*

Cutting

From **BLACK PRINT:**
• Cut 3, 2 x 42-inch inner border strips

From **GREEN PRINT #1:**
• Cut 3, 2 x 42-inch narrow middle border strips

From **BEIGE PRINT #2:**
• Cut 4, 5 x 42-inch wide middle border strips

From **RED PRINT:**
• Cut 4, 3-1/2 x 42-inch outer border strips

Attaching the Borders

Step 1 Attach the 2-inch wide **BLACK** inner border strips.

Step 2 Attach the 2-inch wide **GREEN #1** narrow middle border strips.

Step 3 Attach the 5-inch wide **BEIGE #2** wide middle border strips.

Step 4 Attach the 3-1/2-inch wide **RED** outer border strips.

Appliqué

Cutting

Diagonally piece strips together as needed to get the correct length.

From **GREEN PRINT #2:**
• Cut 1, 1-3/8 x 40-inch **bias** strip
• Cut 1, 1-3/8 x 31-inch **bias** strip
• Cut 2, 1-3/8 x 14-inch **bias** strips
• Cut 2, 1-3/8 x 11-inch **bias** strips

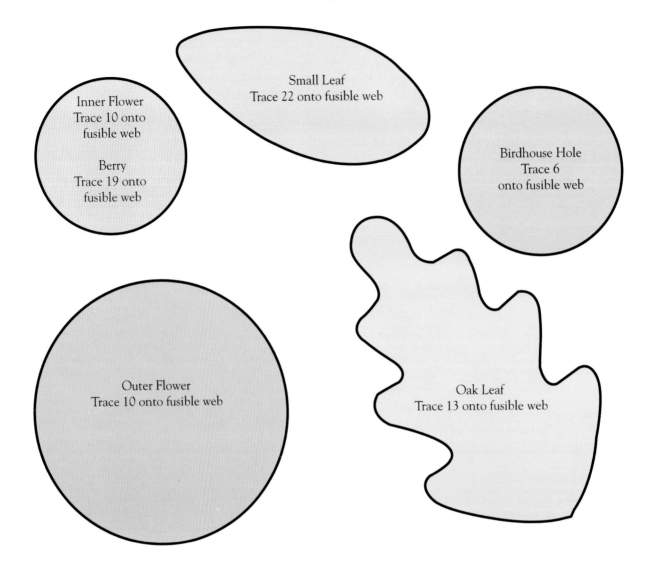

Inner Flower
Trace 10 onto
fusible web

Berry
Trace 19 onto
fusible web

Small Leaf
Trace 22 onto fusible web

Birdhouse Hole
Trace 6
onto fusible web

Outer Flower
Trace 10 onto fusible web

Oak Leaf
Trace 13 onto fusible web

Prepare the Vines

Fold each 1-3/8-inch wide **GREEN #2 bias** strip in half lengthwise with wrong sides together; press. To keep the raw edges aligned, stitch a scant 1/4-inch from the raw edges. Fold the strip in half again so the raw edges are hidden by the first folded edge; press. Hand baste if needed. Set the vine strips aside.

Appliqué - Fusible Web Method

Step 1   Make templates using the shapes above. Position the fusible web, paper side up, over the appliqué shapes. With a pencil, trace the shapes onto fusible web the number of times indicated on the pattern pieces, leaving a small margin between each shape. Cut the shapes apart.

Step 2   Following the manufacturer's instructions, fuse the shapes to the wrong side of the fabric chosen for the appliqués. Let the fabric cool and cut along the traced line. Peel away the paper backing from the fusible web.

Step 3   Referring to the quilt diagram, position the prepared vines and appliqué shapes on the quilt layering them as shown. Fuse the shapes in place and hand baste or pin the vines in place.

Note: *We suggest pinning a rectangle of tear-away stabilizer to the backside of the quilt top to be appliquéd so that it will lay flat when the appliqué is complete. We use the extra-lightweight Easy Tear™ sheets as a stabilizer. When the appliqué is complete, tear away the stabilizer.*

Step 4   We hand stitched the vines in place using matching thread; trim the ends if needed. The other appliqué shapes were machine blanket stitched using Mettler® embroidery thread for the top thread and regular sewing thread in the bobbin. If you like, you could hand blanket stitch around the shapes with pearl cotton. The berries, small leaves, and flower centers were stitched with black thread. The birdhouse holes, flowers, and oak leaves were stitched with gold thread.

Blanket Stitch

Note: *To prevent the hand blanket stitches from "rolling off" the edges of the appliqué shapes, take an extra backstitch in the same place as you made the blanket stitch, going around the outer curves, corners, and points. For straight edges, taking a backstitch every inch is enough.*

Putting It All Together

Trim the backing and batting so they are 4-inches larger than the quilt top. Refer to **Finishing the Quilt** on page 215 for complete instructions.

Binding

Cutting

From **GREEN PRINT #1:**
- Cut 4, 2-3/4 x 42-inch strips

Sew the binding to the quilt using a 3/8-inch seam allowance. This measurement will produce a 1/2-inch wide finished double binding. Refer to **Binding and Diagonal Piecing** on page 215 for complete instructions.

A Garden House
36 x 40-inches

Bittersweet Vine

Great beginnings start small with a small quilt that blends simple piecing with easy appliqué. A central motif—the trailing bittersweet vine—sets the scene for a seasonal autumn accent sized just right for the wall or tabletop.

Bittersweet Vine

28 x 50-inches

Fabrics & Supplies

2/3 yard **BROWN GRID** for runner center

2/3 yard **TAN PRINT** for runner center

3/4 yard **DARK GREEN LEAF PRINT**
for pieced borders, leaf and vine appliqués

1/4 yard **RUST PRINT**
for pieced border and flower appliqués

1/8 yard **DARK RED PRINT** for flower appliqués

1/8 yard **MEDIUM GREEN PRINT** leaf appliqués

3 x 21-inch piece **GOLD PRINT**
for flower center appliqués

5/8 yard **RED FLORAL** for outer border

1/2 yard **DARK GREEN LEAF PRINT** for binding

1-1/2 yards backing fabric

freezer paper for leaf and flower appliqués

lightweight cardboard for circular flower appliqués

template material

quilt batting, at least 34 x 56-inches

Before beginning this project,
read through **Getting Started** on page 210.

Pieced Blocks

Makes 7 blocks

Cutting

From **BROWN GRID:**
- Cut 3, 6-1/2 x 42-inch strips. From the strips cut:
  14, 6-1/2-inch squares

From **TAN PRINT:**
- Cut 3, 6-1/2 x 42-inch strips. From the strips cut:
  7, 6-1/2 x 12-1/2-inch rectangles

Piecing

Step 1 With right sides together, position a
6-1/2-inch **BROWN GRID** square on the left
corner of a 6-1/2 x 12-1/2 inch **TAN** rectangle.
Draw a diagonal line on the square; stitch on the
line. Trim the seam allowance to 1/4-inch; press.
Repeat this process at the opposite corner of
the rectangle.

Make 4

Step 2 Repeat Step 1 reversing the direction of
the drawn sewing line.

Make 3

Step 3 Referring to the runner diagram for block
placement, sew the Step 1 and 2 pieced blocks
together in a row; press. At this point the quilt
center should measure 12-1/2 x 42-1/2-inches.

Appliqué

Cutting the Vine

From **DARK GREEN LEAF PRINT:**
- Cut a 14 x 42-inch strip and set it aside to be used
  for the border strips.
- Cut enough 1-3/8-inch wide **bias** strips to make a
  60-inch long strip.

Note: *Diagonally piece the strips as needed.*

Prepare the Vine

Fold the 1-3/8-inch wide **DARK GREEN LEAF PRINT** strip in half lengthwise with wrong sides together; press. To keep the raw edges aligned, stitch a scant 1/4-inch away from the raw edges. Fold the strip in half again so the raw edges are hidden by the first folded edge; press. Set the prepared vine aside.

Freezer Paper Appliqué Method

Prepare the Leaf A and B and the Flower C Appliqués

With this method of hand appliqué, the freezer paper forms a base around which the appliqués are shaped. The circular flower D and E shapes will be appliquéd using the **Cardboard Appliqué Method**.

Step 1   Make templates using the shapes A, B, and C on page 40. Trace the shapes on the paper side of the freezer paper the number of times indicated on each pattern. Cut out the shapes on the traced lines.

Step 2   With a hot, dry iron, press the coated side of each freezer paper shape onto the wrong side of the fabric chosen for the appliqués. Allow at least 1/2-inch between each shape for seam allowances.

Step 3   Cut out each shape a scant 1/4-inch beyond the edge of the freezer paper pattern.

Step 4   Referring to the runner diagram for placement, position the prepared vine and other appliqué shapes on the runner top, overlapping them as shown. Hand baste the vine in place referring to the basting diagram below; pin the other shapes in place. Basting the vine in this zigzag fashion will hold it nice and flat.

Basting Diagram

Tip: We suggest laying the quilt top on a flat surface for pinning and hand basting the vine in place. Basting the vine makes appliquéing so much easier; no pins to catch your thread.

Step 5   Using matching thread, appliqué the pieces in place, starting with the vine and working from the bottom pieces to the top. Leave a 3/4-inch opening in the leaf and flower shapes for removing the freezer paper. Use the end of your needle to gently loosen the freezer paper from the fabric. Remove the freezer paper and hand stitch the opening closed.

Cardboard Appliqué Method

Prepare the Circular Flower and Flower Center Appliqués

Step 1   Make cardboard templates using the circular flower D and flower center E patterns on page 40.

Step 2   Position the circular flower D template on the wrong side of the fabric chosen for the appliqué and trace around the template 7 times, leaving a 3/4-inch margin around each shape. Remove the template and cut a scant 1/4-inch beyond the drawn lines.

Step 3   To create smooth, round circles, run a line of basting stitches around each circle, placing the stitches halfway between the drawn line and the cut edge of the circle. After basting, keep the needle and thread attached for the next step.

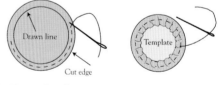

Make 7 circular flowers   Make 7 flower centers

Step 4   Place the cardboard template on the wrong side of the fabric circle and gently pull on the basting stitches, gathering the fabric over the template. When the thread is tight, space the gathers evenly; make a knot to secure the thread. Clip the thread, press the circle, and remove the cardboard template. Continue this process to make 7 circular flowers.

Step 5   Appliqué the circular flowers to the runner top with matching thread. Continue this process to add 7 flower centers.

Borders

Note: *The yardage given allows for the border strips to be cut on the crosswise grain. Diagonally piece the strips together as needed, referring to **Diagonal Piecing** instructions on page 215. Read through **Border** instructions on page 214 for general instructions on adding borders.*

Cutting

From the 14 x 42-inch **DARK GREEN LEAF PRINT** strip cut previously:
- Cut 2 or 3, 2-1/2 x 42-inch strips. Diagonally piece as needed and cut:
  2, 2-1/2 x 42-1/2-inch strips for pieced border
- Cut 2 or 3, 1-1/2 x 42-inch strips. Diagonally piece as needed and cut:
  2, 1-1/2 x 42-1/2-inch strips for pieced border

From **RUST PRINT:**
- Cut 2 or 3, 1-1/2 x 42-inch strips. Diagonally piece as needed and cut:
  2, 1-1/2 x 42-1/2-inch strips for pieced border

From **RED FLORAL:**
- Cut 4, 4-1/2 x 42-inch outer border strips

Attaching the Borders

Step 1 Aligning long edges, sew a 1-1/2 x 42-1/2-inch and 2-1/2 x 42-1/2-inch **DARK GREEN LEAF PRINT** strip to both side edges of a 1-1/2 x 42-1/2-inch **RUST** strip. Refer to **Hints and Helps for Pressing Strip Sets** on page 214. Make 2 pieced border strips, sew them to the sides of the runner center; press.

Make 2

Step 2 Attach the 4-1/2-inch wide **RED FLORAL** outer border strips.

Putting It All Together

Trim the backing and batting so they are 4-inches larger than the runner top. Refer to **Finishing the Quilt** on page 215 for complete instructions.

Binding

Cutting

From **DARK GREEN LEAF PRINT:**
- Cut 5, 2-3/4 x 42-inch strips

Sew the binding to the quilt using a 3/8-inch seam allowance. This measurement will produce a 1/2-inch wide finished double binding. Refer to **Binding and Diagonal Piecing** instructions on page 215 for complete instructions.

Bittersweet Vine Appliqué Templates

The appliqué shapes are reversed for tracing purposes. When the appliqué is finished it will appear as in the diagram.

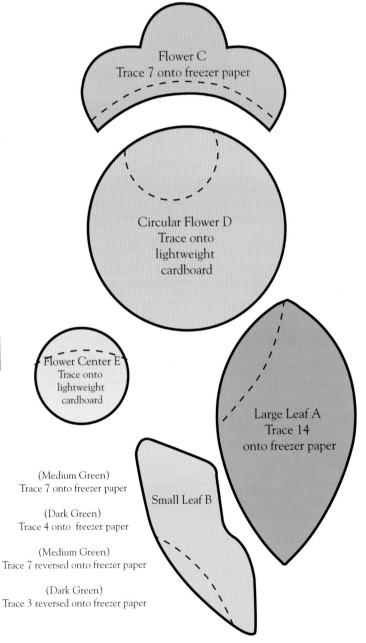

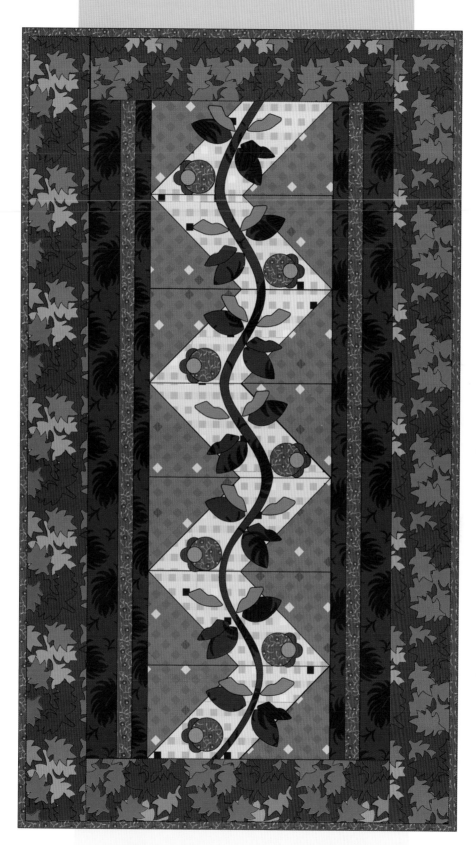

Bittersweet Vine
28 x 50-inches

Bear Paw

Rich multi-colored prints provide strong
contrast for traditional bear paw blocks
set on point in the center of this
dramatic wall quilt. For a weekend of
fun, make the bear paw blocks in
multiples. Set aside a dozen blocks to use
in the corners for a fast finish.

Bear Paw

56-inches square

Fabrics & Supplies

1 yard **TAN PRINT** for background

1/2 yard **GREEN PRINT** for Bear Paw blocks

2/3 yard **RED PRINT #1** for Bear Paw blocks

1 yard **GREEN HOLLY PRINT**
for alternate block, side and corner triangles

3/8 yard **BROWN PRINT** for inner border

1 yard **RED PRINT #2** for outer border

1/2 yard **GREEN PRINT** for binding fabric

3-1/2 yards backing fabric

quilt batting, at least 62-inches square

Before beginning this project,
read through **Getting Started** on page 210.

Bear Paw Blocks

Makes 28 Bear Paw units

Cutting

From **TAN PRINT:**
- Cut 4, 2-7/8 x 42-inch strips
- Cut 2, 2-1/2 x 42-inch strips. From the strips cut:
  28, 2-1/2-inch squares
- Cut 4 more 2-1/2 x 42-inch strips.
  From the strips cut:
  24, 2-1/2 x 6-1/2-inch rectangles

From **GREEN PRINT:**
- Cut 4, 2-7/8 x 42-inch strips
- Cut 1, 2-1/2 x 42-inch strip. From the strip cut:
  8, 2-1/2-inch squares. Set 4 of the squares
  aside to be used in the inner border

From **RED PRINT #1:**
- Cut 4, 4-1/2 x 42-inch strips. From the strips cut:
  28, 4-1/2-inch squares

Piecing

Step 1   With right sides together, layer the
2-7/8 x 42-inch **TAN** and **GREEN PRINT** strips in
pairs. Press together, but do not sew. Cut the layered
strips into squares.

Crosscut 56, 2-7/8-inch squares

Step 2   Cut the layered squares in half diagonally to
make 112 sets of triangles. Stitch 1/4-inch from the
diagonal edge of each pair of triangles; press.

Make 112, 2-1/2-inch triangle-pieced squares

Step 3   Sew the Step 2 triangle-pieced squares
together in pairs; press. Refer to the diagram for
placement of the triangles.

Make 28   Make 28

Unit A   Unit B

Step 4   Sew a 2-1/2-inch **TAN** square to the right edge of a Step 3 Unit B; press. <u>At this point each unit should measure 2-1/2 x 6-1/2-inches.</u>

Make 28

Step 5   Sew a Unit A to the right edge of a 4-1/2-inch **RED** square; press. Sew a Step 4 Unit B to the bottom edge of this unit; press. <u>At this point each unit should measure 6-1/2-inches square.</u>

Unit A

Unit B

Make 28 Bear Paw Units

Step 6   Sew a Bear Paw unit to both side edges of 12 of the 2-1/2 x 6-1/2-inch **TAN** rectangles; press. There will be 4 Bear Paw units remaining which will be used in the outer border. <u>At this point each unit should measure 6-1/2 x 14-1/2-inches.</u>

Make 12

Step 7   Sew a 2-1/2 x 6-1/2-inch **TAN** rectangle to both side edges of a 2-1/2-inch **GREEN** square; press. <u>At this point each unit should measure 2-1/2 x 14-1/2-inches.</u>

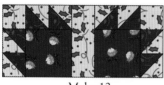

Make 4

Step 8   Sew 8 of the Step 6 units to both side edges of the Step 7 units; press. <u>At this point each block should measure 14-1/2-inches square.</u>

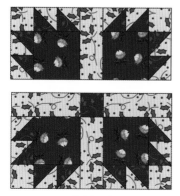

Make 4

Quilt Center

Note: The side and corner triangles are larger than necessary and will be trimmed before the borders are added.

Cutting

From **GREEN HOLLY PRINT**:

- Cut 1, 22 x 42-inch strip. From the strip cut: 1, 22-inch square. Cut the square diagonally into quarters to make 4 side triangles. Also, cut 1, 14-1/2-inch square for the alternate block
- Cut 1, 12 x 42-inch strip. From the strip cut: 2, 12-inch squares. Cut the squares in half diagonally to make 4 corner triangles.

Assembling the Quilt Center

Step 1   Referring to the quilt diagram, sew together the Bear Paw blocks, the alternate block, and the side triangles in diagonal rows. Press the seam allowances in alternating directions by rows so the seams will fit snugly together with less bulk.

Step 2   Pin the rows at the block intersections and sew together; press.

Step 3   Sew the corner triangles to the quilt center; press.

Step 4   Trim away the excess fabric from the side and corner triangles taking care to allow a 1/4-inch seam allowance beyond the corners of each block. Read through **Trimming Side and Corner Triangles** on page 212 for complete instructions.

Borders

*Note: Read through **Border** instructions on page 214 for general instructions on adding borders.*

Cutting

From **BROWN PRINT**:
- Cut 4, 2-1/2 x 42-inch inner border strips

From **RED PRINT #2**:
- Cut 4, 6-1/2 x 42-inch outer border strips

Note: *The 4, 2-1/2-inch* **GREEN PRINT** *corner squares were cut previously in the* **Bear Paw Block** *section.*

Attaching the Borders

Step 1 Attach the top/bottom 2-1/2-inch wide **BROWN** inner border strips. For the side borders, measure the quilt including the seam allowances, but not the top/bottom borders just added. Cut the 2-1/2-inch wide **BROWN** inner border strips to this length. Sew 2-1/2-inch **GREEN PRINT** corner squares to both ends of the **BROWN** side border strips. Sew the border strips to the side edges of the quilt center.

Step 2 To measure for the 6-1/2-inch wide **RED #2** top/bottom outer borders, refer to **Border** instructions on page 214. Subtract 16-inches from this measurement to allow for the Bear Paw blocks and the **TAN** rectangles (cut previously in the Bear Paw Block section). Cut 2 **RED #2** strips to this length.

Step 3 Sew a Bear Paw block to each end of the Step 2, 6-1/2-inch wide **RED #2** strips; press. Sew a 2-1/2 x 6-1/2-inch **TAN** rectangle to each end of the strips; press. Sew the border strips to the top/bottom edges of the quilt; press.

Step 4 To measure for the 6-1/2-inch wide **RED #2** side outer borders, refer to **Border** instructions on page 214. Subtract 28-inches from this measurement to allow for the Step 6 Bear Paw Block/**TAN** rectangle unit at each end. Cut 2 **RED #2** strips to this length.

Step 5 Sew a Bear Paw block/**TAN** rectangle unit to each end of the **RED #2** strips; press. Sew the border strips to the side edges of the quilt; press.

Putting It All Together

Cut the 3-1/2 yard length of backing fabric in half crosswise to make 2, 1-3/4 yard lengths. Refer to **Finishing the Quilt** on page 215 for complete instructions.

Binding

Cutting

From **GREEN PRINT:**
• Cut 6, 2-3/4 x 42-inch strips

Sew the binding to the quilt using a 3/8-inch seam allowance. This measurement will produce a 1/2-inch wide finished double binding. Refer to **Binding** and **Diagonal Piecing** on page 215 for complete instructions.

Bear Paw

56-inches square

Holiday Stars

Blue

Spark some fireworks with a quilt
featuring fabrics in Fourth of July and
summertime favorite colors—red, white,
and blue. Use Holiday Stars as a
backdrop for a party that starts with
hand-delivered firecracker invitations
made from mailing tubes painted red and
sprinkled with gold star stickers.

Holiday Stars

Blue

65-inches square

Fabrics & Supplies

1-1/4 yards **BLUE PRINT** for blocks, lattice post squares, and sawtooth border

1-3/4 yards **BEIGE PRINT** for background, middle border, and sawtooth border

5/8 yard **GOLD PRINT** for blocks and middle border

1-5/8 yards **RED PRINT #1** for blocks and outer border

2/3 yard **RED PRINT #2** for lattice segments

2/3 yard **BLUE PLAID** for binding (cut on the bias)

4 yards backing fabric

quilt batting, at least 71-inches square

Before beginning this project, read through **Getting Started** on page 210.

Star Blocks

Makes 9 blocks

Cutting

From **BLUE PRINT:**
- Cut 5, 2-1/2 x 42-inch strips. From the strips cut: 72, 2-1/2-inch squares
- Cut 3 more 2-1/2 x 42-inch strips

From **BEIGE PRINT:**
- Cut 8, 2-1/2 x 42-inch strips. From the strips cut: 72, 2-1/2 x 4-1/2-inch rectangles
- Cut 3 more 2-1/2 x 42-inch strips

From **GOLD PRINT:**
- Cut 4, 2-1/2 x 42-inch strips. From the strips cut: 36, 2-1/2 x 4-1/2-inch rectangles

From **RED PRINT #1:**
- Cut 1, 4-1/2 x 42-inch strip. From the strip cut: 9, 4-1/2-inch squares

Piecing

Step 1   With right sides together, position a 2-1/2-inch **BLUE** square on the corner of a 2-1/2 x 4-1/2-inch **BEIGE** rectangle. Draw a diagonal line on the square and stitch on the line. Trim the seam allowance to 1/4-inch; press. Repeat this process at the opposite corner of the rectangle.

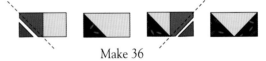

Make 36

Step 2   Sew a 2-1/2 x 4-1/2-inch **GOLD** rectangle to the bottom edge of each of the Step 1 units; press.

Make 36

Step 3   Aligning long edges, sew together the 2-1/2 x 42-inch **BLUE** and **BEIGE** strips in pairs; press. Make a total of 3 strip sets. Cut the strip sets into segments.

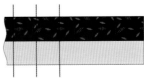

Crosscut 36, 2-1/2-inch wide segments

Step 4   Sew a 2-1/2 x 4-1/2-inch **BEIGE** rectangle to the bottom edge of each Step 3 segment; press.

Make 36

Step 5   Sew Step 2 units to both side edges of a 4-1/2-inch **RED #1** square; press. <u>At this point each unit should measure 4-1/2 x 12-1/2-inches.</u>

Make 9

Step 6   Sew Step 4 units to both side edges of a Step 2 unit; press. <u>At this point each unit should measure 4-1/2 x 12-1/2-inches.</u>

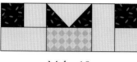

Make 18

Step 7   Sew Step 6 units to both side edges of a Step 5 unit; press. <u>At this point each star block should measure 12-1/2-inches square.</u>

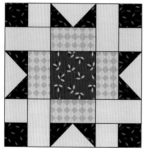

Make 9

Quilt Center

Cutting

From RED PRINT #2:
- Cut 8, 2-1/2 x 42-inch strips. From the strips cut: 24, 2-1/2 x 12-1/2-inch lattice segments

From BLUE PRINT:
- Cut 1, 2-1/2 x 42-inch strip. From the strip cut: 16, 2-1/2-inch lattice post squares

Assembling and Attaching the Lattice Strips

Step 1   Sew together 3 of the 2-1/2 x 12-1/2-inch **RED #2** lattice segments and 4 of the 2-1/2-inch **BLUE** lattice posts; press. Make 4 lattice strips. <u>At this point each lattice strip should measure 2-1/2 x 44-1/2-inches.</u>

Step 2   Sew together 3 of the star blocks and 4 of the 2-1/2 x 12-1/2-inch **RED #2** lattice segments; press. Make 3 block rows. <u>At this point each block row should measure 12-1/2 x 44-1/2-inches.</u>

Step 3   Pin the block rows and lattice strips together at the block intersections. Sew the strips together; press. <u>At this point the quilt center should measure 44-1/2-inches square.</u>

Borders

Note: *The yardage given allows for the border strips to be cut on the crosswise grain. Diagonally piece the strips as needed, referring to* **Diagonal Piecing** *instructions on page 215. Read through* **Border** *instructions on page 214 general instructions on adding borders.*

Cutting

From BEIGE PRINT:
- Cut 5, 2-1/2 x 42-inch inner border strips
- Cut 4, 2-7/8 x 42-inch strips for sawtooth border
- Cut 1, 2-1/2 x 42-inch strip. From the strip cut: 4, 2-1/2-inch squares for sawtooth border corner squares

From **BLUE PRINT:**
- Cut 4, 2-7/8 x 42-inch strips for sawtooth border

From **GOLD PRINT:**
- Cut 6, 1 x 42-inch middle border strips

From **RED PRINT #1:**
- Cut 7, 6-1/2 x 42-inch outer border strips

Attaching the Borders

Step 1   Attach the 2-1/2-inch wide **BEIGE** inner border strips.

Step 2   With right sides together, layer the 2-7/8 x 42-inch **BEIGE** and **BLUE** strips in pairs. Press together, but do not sew. Cut the layered strips into squares. Cut the layered squares in half diagonally to make 96 sets of triangles. Stitch 1/4-inch from the diagonal edge of each pair of triangles; press.

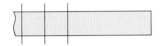

Crosscut 48, 2-7/8-inch squares

Make 96, 2-1/2-inch triangle-pieced squares

Step 3   Sew 24 triangle-pieced squares together for each of the top/bottom sawtooth borders, as shown in the quilt diagram. Notice how the sawtooth border changes direction from the center out. Sew the border strips to the top/bottom edges of the quilt center; press.

Note: If the completed sawtooth border is too long or too short, adjust seams in many places rather than trying to make up the difference in just a few places. You must match the center of the border to the center of the quilt and adjust the seams going in either direction.

Step 4   Sew 24 triangle-pieced squares together for each side sawtooth border; press. Notice how the sawtooth border changes direction from the center out. Sew 2-1/2-inch **BEIGE** corner squares to both ends of the border strips; press. Sew the border strips to the side edges of the quilt; press.

Step 5   Attach the 1-inch wide **GOLD** middle border strips.

Step 6   Attach the 6-1/2-inch wide **RED #1** outer border strips.

Putting It All Together

Cut the 4 yard length of backing fabric in half crosswise to make 2, 2 yard lengths. Refer to **Finishing the Quilt** on page 215 for complete instructions.

Binding

Cutting

From **BLUE PLAID:**
- Cut enough 2-3/4-inch wide **bias** strips to make a 275-inch long strip.

OR

- Cut the remaining quilt fabrics into 2-3/4-inch wide pieces to create an interesting pieced binding. Diagonally piece the strips together.

Sew the binding to the quilt using a 3/8-inch seam allowance. This measurement will produce a 1/2-inch wide finished double binding. Refer to **Binding and Diagonal Piecing** on page 215 for complete instructions.

Holiday Stars
Blue
65-inches square

Holiday Stars

Green

65-inches square

Fabrics & Supplies

1-1/4 yards **GREEN PRINT**
for blocks, lattice posts, and sawtooth border

1-3/4 yards **BEIGE PRINT** for background,
middle border, and sawtooth border

5/8 yard **GOLD PRINT**
for blocks and middle border

1-5/8 yards **RED PRINT**
for blocks and outer border

2/3 yard **CHESTNUT FLORAL**
for lattice segments

2/3 yard **GREEN PLAID**
for binding (cut on the bias)

4 yards backing fabric

quilt batting, at least 71-inches square

Before beginning this project,
read through **Getting Started** on page 210.

Star Blocks

Makes 9 blocks

Cutting

From **GREEN PRINT:**
- Cut 5, 2-1/2 x 42-inch strips. From the strips cut:
  72, 2-1/2-inch squares
- Cut 3 more 2-1/2 x 42-inch strips

From **BEIGE PRINT:**
- Cut 8, 2-1/2 x 42-inch strips. From the strips cut:
  72, 2-1/2 x 4-1/2-inch rectangles
- Cut 3 more 2-1/2 x 42-inch strips

From **GOLD PRINT:**
- Cut 4, 2-1/2 x 42-inch strips. From the strips cut:
  36, 2-1/2 x 4-1/2-inch rectangles

From **RED PRINT:**
- Cut 1, 4-1/2 x 42-inch strip. From the strip cut:
  9, 4-1/2-inch squares

Piecing

Step 1 With right sides together, position a 2-1/2-inch **GREEN** square on the corner of a 2-1/2 x 4-1/2-inch **BEIGE** rectangle. Draw a diagonal line on the square and stitch on the line. Trim the seam allowance to 1/4-inch; press. Repeat this process at the opposite corner of the rectangle.

Make 36

Step 2 Sew a 2-1/2 x 4-1/2-inch **GOLD** rectangle to the bottom edge of each of the Step 1 units; press.

Make 36

Step 3 Aligning long edges, sew the 2-1/2 x 42-inch **GREEN** and **BEIGE** strips together in pairs. Make a total of 3 strip sets. Cut the strip sets into segments.

Crosscut 36, 2-1/2-inch wide segments

Step 4 Sew a 2-1/2 x 4-1/2-inch **BEIGE** rectangle to the bottom edge of each Step 3 segment; press.

Make 36

Step 5 Sew Step 2 units to both side edges of a 4-1/2-inch **RED** square; press. At this point each unit should measure 4-1/2 x 12-1/2-inches.

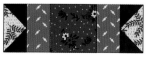

Make 9

Step 6 Sew Step 4 units to both side edges of a Step 2 unit; press. At this point each unit should measure 4-1/2 x 12-1/2-inches.

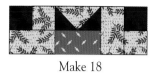

Make 18

Step 7 Sew Step 6 units to both side edges of a Step 5 unit; press. At this point each star block should measure 12-1/2-inches square.

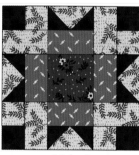

Make 9

Quilt Center

Cutting

From **CHESTNUT FLORAL**:
• Cut 8, 2-1/2 x 42-inch strips. From the strips cut: 24, 2-1/2 x 12-1/2-inch lattice segments

From **GREEN PRINT**:
• Cut 1, 2-1/2 x 42-inch strip. From the strip cut: 16, 2-1/2-inch lattice post squares

Assembling and Attaching the Lattice Strips

Step 1 Sew together 3 of the 2-1/2 x 12-1/2-inch **CHESTNUT** lattice segments and 4 of the 2-1/2-inch **GREEN** lattice post squares. Press the seam allowances toward the lattice segments. Make 4 lattice strips. At this point each lattice strip should measure 2-1/2 x 44-1/2-inches.

Step 2 Sew together 3 of the star blocks, and 4 of the 2-1/2 x 12-1/2-inch **CHESTNUT** lattice segments. Press the seam allowances toward the lattice segments. Make 3 block rows. At this point each block row should measure 12-1/2 x 44-1/2-inches.

Step 3   Pin the block rows and lattice strips together at the block intersections. Sew the strips together; press. <u>At this point the quilt center should measure 44-1/2-inches square.</u>

Borders

Note: *The yardage given allows for the border strips to be cut on the crosswise grain. Diagonally piece the strips as needed, referring to* **Diagonal Piecing** *instructions on page 215. Read through* **Border** *instructions on page 214 for general instructions on adding borders.*

Cutting

From **BEIGE PRINT:**
- Cut 5, 2-1/2 x 42-inch inner border strips
- Cut 4, 2-7/8 x 42-inch strips for sawtooth border
- Cut 1, 2-1/2 x 42-inch strip. From the strip cut: 4, 2-1/2-inch squares for sawtooth border corner squares

From **GREEN PRINT:**
- Cut 4, 2-7/8 x 42-inch strips for sawtooth border

From **GOLD PRINT:**
- Cut 6, 1 x 42-inch middle border strips

From **RED PRINT:**
- Cut 7, 6-1/2 x 42-inch outer border strips

Attaching the Borders

Step 1   Attach the 2-1/2-inch wide **BEIGE** inner border strips.

Step 2   With right sides together, layer the 2-7/8 x 42-inch **BEIGE** and **GREEN** strips in pairs. Press together, but do not sew. Cut the layered strips into squares. Cut the layered squares in half diagonally to make 96 sets of triangles. Stitch 1/4-inch from the diagonal edge of each pair of triangles; press.

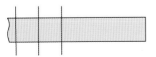

Crosscut 48, 2-7/8-inch squares

Make 96, 2-1/2-inch triangle-pieced squares

Step 3   Sew 24 triangle-pieced squares together for each of the top/bottom sawtooth borders, as shown in the quilt diagram. Notice how the sawtooth border changes direction from the center out. Sew the border strips to the top/bottom edges of the quilt center; press.

Note: *If the completed sawtooth border is too long or too short, adjust seams in many places rather than trying to make up the difference in just a few places. You must match the center of the border to the center of the quilt and adjust the seams going in either direction.*

Step 4   Sew 24 triangle-pieced squares together for each side sawtooth border; press. Notice how the sawtooth border changes direction from the center out. Sew 2-1/2-inch **BEIGE** corner squares to both ends of the border strips; press. Sew the border strips to the side edges of the quilt; press.

Step 5   Attach the 1-inch wide **GOLD** middle border strips.

Step 6   Attach the 6-1/2-inch wide **RED** outer border strips.

Putting It All Together

Cut the 4 yard length of backing fabric in half crosswise to make 2, 2 yard lengths. Refer to **Finishing the Quilt** on page 215 for complete instructions.

Binding

Cutting

From **GREEN PLAID:**
- Cut enough 2-3/4-inch wide **bias** strips to make a 275-inch long strip.

Sew the binding to the quilt using a 3/8-inch seam allowance. This measurement will produce a 1/2-inch wide finished double binding. Refer to **Binding and Diagonal Piecing** on page 215 for complete instructions.

Holiday Stars
Green
65-inches square

High Country Pinwheels

Blue

Soak up some summer sunshine with a patchwork of spinning pinwheels. In High Country Pinwheels, pleasing fabric colors are combined to form blocks that have visual movement. The floral border, repeated in the quilt center, ties it all together.

High Country Pinwheels

Blue

56-inches square

Fabrics & Supplies

7/8 yard **BLUE CHECK** for pinwheels

1/2 yard **BEIGE PRINT** for background

1-7/8 yards **BLUE PRINT**
for pinwheels and outer border

1-1/8 yards **LARGE FLORAL**
for quilt center and middle border

1/2 yard **ROSE PRINT**
for inner border and corner squares

5/8 yard **BLUE PRINT** for binding

3-1/2 yards backing fabric

quilt batting, at least 62-inches square

Before beginning this project,
read through **Getting Started** on page 210.

Pinwheel Blocks

Makes 4 blocks

Cutting

From **BLUE CHECK:**
- Cut 2, 4-7/8 x 42-inch strips
- Cut 1, 4-7/8 x 12-inch strip
- Cut 2, 4-1/2 x 42-inch strips. From the strips cut:
  16, 4-1/2 inch squares

From **BEIGE PRINT:**
- Cut 1, 4-7/8 x 42-inch strip
- Cut 2, 4-1/2 x 42-inch strips. From the strips cut:
  8, 4-1/2 x 8-1/2-inch rectangles

From **BLUE PRINT:**
- Cut 1, 4-7/8 x 42-inch strip
- Cut 2, 4-1/2 x 42-inch strips. From the strips cut:
  16, 4-1/2-inch squares

From **LARGE FLORAL:**
- Cut 1, 4-7/8 x 12-inch strip
- Cut 2, 4-1/2 x 42-inch strips. From the strips cut:
  8, 4-1/2 x 8-1/2-inch rectangles

Piecing

Step 1   With right sides together, layer a
4-7/8 x 42-inch **BLUE CHECK** and **BEIGE** strip
together. Press together, but do not sew. Cut the
layered strip into squares. Cut the layered squares in
half diagonally to make 12 sets of triangles. Stitch
1/4-inch from the diagonal edge of each pair of
triangles; press.

Crosscut 6, 4-7/8-inch squares

Make 12, 4-1/2-inch triangle-pieced squares

Step 2   With right sides together, layer a
4-7/8 x 42-inch **BLUE CHECK** and **BLUE
PRINT** strip together. Press together, but do not
sew. Cut the layered strip into squares. Cut the

layered squares in half diagonally to make 16 sets of triangles. Stitch 1/4-inch from the diagonal edge of each pair of triangles; press.

Crosscut 8, 4-7/8-inch squares

Make 16, 4-1/2-inch triangle-pieced squares

Step 3 Sew the Step 2 triangle-pieced squares together in pairs; press. Sew the pairs together; press. <u>At this point each pinwheel unit should measure 8-1/2-inches square.</u>

Make 8   Make 4

Step 4 With right sides together, layer a 4-7/8 x 12-inch **LARGE FLORAL** and **BLUE CHECK** strip together. Press together, but do not sew. Cut the layered strip into squares. Cut the layered squares in half diagonally to make 4 sets of triangles. Stitch 1/4-inch from the diagonal edge of each pair of triangles; press.

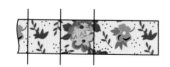

Crosscut 2, 4-7/8-inch squares

Make 4, 4-1/2-inch triangle-pieced squares

Step 5 With right sides together, position a 4-1/2-inch **BLUE PRINT** square on the left corner of a 4-1/2 x 8-1/2-inch **LARGE FLORAL** rectangle. Draw a diagonal line on the square and stitch on the line. Trim the seam allowances

to 1/4-inch; press. Position a 4-1/2-inch **BLUE CHECK** square on the right corner of the rectangle. Draw a diagonal line on the square; stitch, trim, and press.

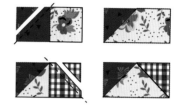

Make 8

Step 6 With right sides together, position a 4-1/2-inch **BLUE PRINT** square on the left corner of a 4-1/2 x 8-1/2-inch **BEIGE** rectangle. Draw a diagonal line on the square; stitch, trim, and press. Position a 4-1/2-inch **BLUE CHECK** square on the right corner of the rectangle. Draw a diagonal line on the square; stitch, trim, and press.

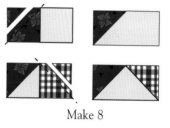

Make 8

Note: Refer to the block diagram for color placement. Each block is made up of a Row 1, Row 2, and Row 3.

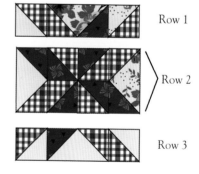

Block Diagram

Step 7 To make Row 1, sew together a Step 1 triangle-pieced square, a Step 5 unit, and a Step 4 triangle-pieced square as shown; press. <u>At this point each Row 1 should measure 4-1/2 x 16-1/2-inches.</u>

Make 4

Step 8 To make Row 2, sew together a Step 5 unit, a Step 6 unit, and a Step 3 unit as shown; press. <u>At this point each Row 2 should measure 8-1/2 x 16-1/2-inches.</u>

Row 2

Make 4

Step 9 To make Row 3, sew together 2 of the Step 1 triangle-pieced squares and a Step 6 unit as shown; press. <u>At this point each Row 3 should measure 4-1/2 x 16-1/2-inches.</u>

Row 3

Make 4

Step 10 Sew together the 3 rows to make each pinwheel block; press. <u>At this point each pinwheel block should measure 16-1/2 inches square.</u>

Step 11 Referring to the quilt diagram, sew the blocks together; press.

Borders

Note: The yardage given allows for the border strips to be cut on the crosswise grain. Diagonally piece the strips as needed, referring to **Diagonal Piecing** *instructions on page 215. Read through* **Borders** *on page 214 for general instructions on adding borders.*

Cutting

From **ROSE PRINT:**
• Cut 4, 2-1/2 x 42-inch inner border strips
• Cut 4, 4-1/2-inch corner squares

From **LARGE FLORAL:**
• Cut 4, 4-1/2 x 42-inch middle border strips

From **BLUE PRINT:**
• Cut 6, 6-1/2 x 42-inch outer border strips

Attaching the Borders

Step 1 Attach the 2-1/2-inch wide **ROSE** inner border strips.

Step 2 Attach the 4-1/2-inch wide **LARGE FLORAL** top/bottom middle border strips. For the side borders, measure the quilt including the seam allowances, but not the top/bottom borders just added. Cut the 4-1/2-inch wide **LARGE FLORAL** side middle border strips to this length. Sew 4-1/2-inch **ROSE** corner squares to both ends of the border strips; press. Sew the strips to the side edges of the quilt center.

Step 3 Attach the 6-1/2-inch wide **BLUE PRINT** outer border strips.

Putting It All Together

Cut the 3-1/2 yard length of backing in half crosswise to make 2, 1-3/4 yard lengths. Refer to **Finishing the Quilt** on page 215 for complete instructions.

Binding

Cutting

From **BLUE PRINT:**
• Cut 6, 2-3/4 x 42-inch strips

Sew the binding to the quilt using a 3/8-inch seam allowance. This measurement will produce a 1/2-inch wide finished double binding. Refer to **Binding and Diagonal Piecing** instructions on page 215 for complete instructions.

High Country Pinwheels
Blue
56-inches square

High Country Pinwheels
Christmas

56-inches square

Fabrics & Supplies

7/8 yard **GREEN CHECK** for pinwheels

1/2 yard **BEIGE PRINT** for background

1-7/8 yards **RED PRINT**
for pinwheels and outer border

1-1/8 yards **LARGE GREEN FLORAL**
for quilt center and middle border

1/2 yard **BLACK PRINT**
for inner border and corner squares

2/3 yard **GREEN CHECK**
for binding (cut on the bias)

3-1/2 yards backing fabric

quilt batting, at least 62-inches square

Before beginning this project,
read through **Getting Started** on page 210.

Pinwheel Blocks

Makes 4 blocks

Cutting

From **GREEN CHECK:**
- Cut 2, 4-7/8 x 42-inch strips
- Cut 1, 4-7/8 x 12-inch strip
- Cut 2, 4-1/2 x 42-inch strips. From the strips cut:
  16, 4-1/2 inch squares

From **BEIGE PRINT:**
- Cut 1, 4-7/8 x 42-inch strip
- Cut 2, 4-1/2 x 42-inch strips. From the strips cut:
  8, 4-1/2 x 8-1/2-inch rectangles

From **RED PRINT:**
- Cut 1, 4-7/8 x 42-inch strip
- Cut 2, 4-1/2 x 42-inch strips. From the strips cut:
  16, 4-1/2-inch squares

From **LARGE GREEN FLORAL:**
- Cut 1, 4-7/8 x 12-inch strip
- Cut 2, 4-1/2 x 42-inch strips. From the strips cut:
  8, 4-1/2 x 8-1/2-inch rectangles

Piecing

Step 1   With right sides together, layer a 4-7/8 x 42-inch **GREEN CHECK** and **BEIGE** strip together. Press together, but do not sew. Cut the layered strip into squares. Cut the layered squares in half diagonally to make 12 sets of triangles. Stitch 1/4-inch from the diagonal edge of each pair of triangles; press.

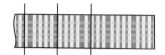

Crosscut 6, 4-7/8-inch squares

Make 12, 4-1/2-inch triangle-pieced squares

Step 2   With right sides together, layer a 4-7/8 x 42-inch **GREEN CHECK** and **RED** strip together. Press together, but do not sew. Cut the layered strip into squares. Cut the layered squares in half diagonally to make 16 sets of triangles. Stitch 1/4-inch from the diagonal edge of each pair of triangles; press.

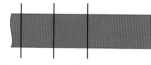

Crosscut 8, 4-7/8-inch squares

Make 16, 4-1/2-inch triangle-pieced squares

Step 3   Sew the Step 2 triangle-pieced squares together in pairs; press. Sew the pairs together; press. At this point each pinwheel unit should measure 8-1/2-inches square.

Make 8

Make 4

Step 4   With right sides together, layer a 4-7/8 x 12-inch **LARGE GREEN FLORAL** and **GREEN CHECK** strip together. Press together, but do not sew. Cut the layered strip into squares. Cut the layered squares in half diagonally to make 4 sets of triangles. Stitch 1/4-inch from the diagonal edge of each pair of triangles; press.

Crosscut 2, 4-7/8-inch squares

Make 4, 4-1/2-inch triangle-pieced squares

Step 5   With right sides together, position a 4-1/2-inch **RED** square on the left corner of a 4-1/2 x 8-1/2-inch **LARGE GREEN FLORAL** rectangle. Draw a diagonal line on the square and stitch on the line. Trim the seam allowances to 1/4-inch; press. Position a 4-1/2-inch **GREEN CHECK** square on the right corner of the rectangle. Draw a diagonal line on the square; stitch, trim, and press.

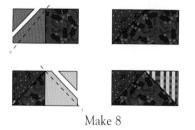

Make 8

Step 6   With right sides together, position a 4-1/2-inch **RED** square on the left corner of a 4-1/2 x 8-1/2-inch **BEIGE** rectangle. Draw a diagonal line on the square; stitch, trim, and press. Position a 4-1/2-inch **GREEN CHECK** square on the right corner of the rectangle. Draw a diagonal line on the square; stitch, trim, and press.

Make 8

Note: *Refer to the block diagram for color placement. Each block is made up of a Row 1, Row 2, and Row 3.*

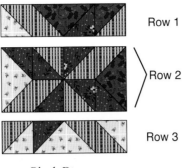

Block Diagram

Step 7 To make Row 1, sew together a Step 1 triangle-pieced square, a Step 5 unit, and a Step 4 triangle-pieced square as shown; press. <u>At this point each Row 1 should measure 4-1/2 x 16-1/2-inches.</u>

Make 4

Step 8 To make Row 2, sew together a Step 5 unit, a Step 6 unit, and a Step 3 unit as shown; press. <u>At this point each Row 2 should measure 8-1/2 x 16-1/2-inches.</u>

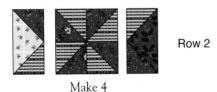

Make 4

Step 9 To make Row 3, sew together 2 of the Step 1 triangle-pieced squares and a Step 6 unit as shown; press. <u>At this point each Row 3 should measure 4-1/2 x 16-1/2-inches.</u>

Make 4

Step 10 Sew together the 3 rows to make each pinwheel block; press. <u>At this point each pinwheel block should measure 16-1/2 inches square.</u>

Step 11 Referring to the quilt diagram, sew the blocks together; press.

Borders

Note: *The yardage given allows for the border strips to be cut on the crosswise grain. Diagonally piece the strips as needed, referring to* **Diagonal Piecing** *instructions on page 215. Read through* **Borders** *on page 214 for general instructions on adding borders.*

Cutting

From **BLACK PRINT:**
- Cut 4, 2-1/2 x 42-inch inner border strips
- Cut 4, 4-1/2-inch corner squares

From **LARGE GREEN FLORAL:**
- Cut 4, 4-1/2 x 42-inch middle border strips

From **RED PRINT:**
- Cut 6, 6-1/2 x 42-inch outer border strips

Attaching the Borders

Step 1 Attach the 2-1/2-inch wide **BLACK** inner border strips.

Step 2 Attach the 4-1/2-inch wide **LARGE GREEN FLORAL** top/bottom middle border strips. For the side borders, measure the quilt including the seam allowances, but not the top/bottom borders just added. Cut the 4-1/2-inch wide **LARGE GREEN FLORAL** side middle border strips to this length. Sew 4-1/2-inch **BLACK** corner squares to both ends of the border strips; press. Sew the strips to the side edges of the quilt center.

Step 3 Attach the 6-1/2-inch wide **RED** outer border strips.

Putting It All Together

Cut the 3-1/2 yard length of backing in half crosswise to make 2, 1-3/4 yard lengths. Refer to **Finishing the Quilt** on page 215 for complete instructions.

Binding

Cutting

From **GREEN CHECK:**
- Cut enough 2-3/4-inch wide **bias** strips to make a 240-inch long strip.

Sew the binding to the quilt using a 3/8-inch seam allowance. This measurement will produce a 1/2-inch wide finished double binding. Refer to **Binding and Diagonal Piecing** instructions on page 215 for complete instructions.

High Country Pinwheels
Christmas
56-inches square

Casual

COMFORTS

iscover the joys of creating your own safe haven filled with soul-satisfying comforts. Since simplicity is at the heart of cottage-style decorating, on the pages that follow you'll find eight cozy cottage throws designed to help you surround yourself with the serenity you've been seeking—the essence of country-cottage style!

Oh Baby, Baby

Simple piecing, soft colors and a gentle
quilting design are the A, B, Cs of a
quilt just right for a baby's room or a
charming cottage accent.

Oh Baby, Baby

47 x 55-inches

Fabrics & Supplies

1-1/4 yards **GREEN PRINT**
for blocks, lattice posts, borders, and corner squares

1-7/8 yards **BEIGE PRINT**
for background and lattice strips

1-1/2 yards **GREEN/BEIGE PLAID** for borders
and corner squares (cut lengthwise grain)

Note: *Cutting the border strips on the lengthwise grain will eliminate the need for piecing and matching the plaid border strips.*

OR

1 yard **GREEN/BEIGE PLAID**
for borders and corner squares (cut crosswise grain)

1/2 yard **GREEN PRINT** for binding

3 yards backing fabric

quilt batting, at least 53 x 61-inches

Before beginning this project,
read through **Getting Started** on page 210.

Pieced Blocks

Makes 20 blocks

Cutting

From **GREEN PRINT:**
• Cut 12, 1-1/2 x 42-inch strips

From **BEIGE PRINT:**
• Cut 1, 5-1/2 x 42-inch strip
• Cut 6, 3-1/2 x 42-inch strips
• Cut 4, 2-1/2 x 42-inch strips
• Cut 6, 1-1/2 x 42-inch strips

Piecing

Note: *The pieced blocks are made up of strip sets. Refer to* **Hints and Helps for Pressing Strip Sets** *on page 214.*

Step 1   Aligning long edges, sew a 3-1/2-inch wide **BEIGE** strip to both side edges of a 1-1/2-inch wide **GREEN** strip; press. Make 2 strip sets. Cut the strip sets into segments.

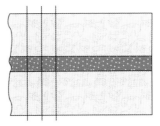

Strip Set A
Crosscut 40, 1-1/2-inch wide segments

Step 2   Aligning long edges, sew together 2 of the 2-1/2-inch wide **BEIGE** strips, 2 of the 1-1/2-inch wide **GREEN** strips, and 1 of the 1-1/2-inch wide **BEIGE** strips; press. Make 2 strip sets. Cut the strip sets into segments.

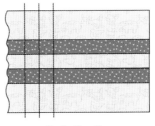

Strip Set B
Crosscut 40, 1-1/2-inch wide segments

Step 3 Aligning long edges, sew together 2 of the 1-1/2-inch wide **BEIGE** strips, 2 of the 1-1/2-inch wide **GREEN** strips, and 1 of the 3-1/2-inch wide **BEIGE** strips; press. Make 2 strip sets. Cut the strip sets into segments.

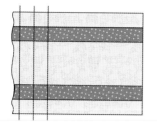

Strip Set C
Crosscut 40, 1-1/2-inch wide segments

Step 4 Aligning long edges, sew a 1-1/2-inch wide **GREEN** strip to both side edges of the 5-1/2-inch wide **BEIGE** strip; press. Cut the strip set into segments.

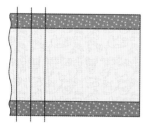

Strip Set D
Crosscut 40, 1-1/2-inch wide segments

Step 5 Sew the Step 1, 2, 3, and 4 strip sets together to make a pieced block; press. <u>At this point each pieced block should measure 7-1/2-inches square.</u>

A B C D C B A

Make 20

Quilt Center

Note: *The yardage given allows for the lattice strips to be cut on the crosswise grain.*

Cutting

From **BEIGE PRINT**:
• Cut 10, 1-1/2 x 42-inch strips.
    From the strips cut:
    49, 1-1/2 x 7-1/2-inch lattice strips

From **GREEN PRINT**:
• Cut 2, 1-1/2 x 42-inch strips. From the strips cut:
    30, 1-1/2-inch lattice posts

Piecing

Step 1 Referring to the quilt diagram, sew together 5 of the 1-1/2-inch **GREEN** lattice posts and 4 of the 1-1/2 x 7-1/2-inch **BEIGE** lattice strips; press. Make 6 lattice strips.

Step 2 Referring to the quilt diagram, sew together 5 of the 1-1/2 x 7-1/2-inch **BEIGE** lattice strips and 4 of the pieced blocks; press. Make 5 block rows.

Step 3 Referring to the quilt diagram, pin the lattice strips and the block rows together at the block intersections. Sew the strips together; press. <u>At this point the quilt center should measure 33-1/2 x 41-1/2-inches.</u>

Borders

Note: *The yardage given allows for the border strips to be cut on the lengthwise grain (a couple extra inches are allowed for trimming). Cutting the strips on the lengthwise grain will eliminate the need for piecing and matching the plaid border strips. If you are cutting your borders on the crosswise grain, you will need to diagonally piece the strips as needed referring to* **Diagonal Piecing** *instructions on page 215. Read through* **Border** *instructions on page 214 for general instructions on adding borders.*

Cutting

From **GREEN PRINT:**
- Cut 5, 2-1/2 x 42-inch middle border strips.
    From one of the strips cut:
    4, 2-1/2-inch corner squares
- Cut 4, 3-1/2-inch corner squares

From **GREEN/BEIGE PLAID** (cut on the lengthwise grain):
- Cut 2, 3-1/2 x 52-inch side outer border strips
- Cut 2, 3-1/2 x 43-inch top/bottom outer border strips
- Cut 2, 2-1/2 x 43-inch side inner border strips
- Cut 2, 2-1/2 x 35-inch top/bottom inner border strips
- Cut 4, 2-1/2-inch corner squares

OR

From **GREEN/BEIGE PLAID** (cut on the crosswise grain):
- Cut 4, 2-1/2 x 42-inch inner border strips.
    From one of the strips cut:
    4, 2-1/2-inch corner squares
- Cut 5, 3-1/2 x 42-inch outer border strips

Attaching the Borders

Step 1   Attach the top/bottom 2-1/2-inch wide **GREEN/BEIGE PLAID** inner border strips. For the side borders, measure the quilt including the seam allowances, but not the top/bottom borders just added. Cut the 2-1/2-inch wide **GREEN/BEIGE PLAID** side inner border strips to this length. Sew the 2-1/2-inch **GREEN** corner squares to both ends of the border strips; press. Sew the strips to the side edges of the quilt center.

Step 2   Attach the top/bottom 2-1/2-inch wide **GREEN** middle border strips. For the side borders, measure the quilt including the seam allowances, but not the top/bottom borders just added. Cut the 2-1/2-inch wide **GREEN** side middle border strips to this length. Sew the 2-1/2-inch **GREEN/BEIGE PLAID** corner squares to both ends of the border strips; press. Sew the strips to the side edges of the quilt center.

Step 3   Attach the top/bottom 3-1/2-inch wide **GREEN/BEIGE PLAID** outer border strips. For the side borders, measure the quilt including the seam allowances, but not the top/bottom borders just added. Cut the 3-1/2-inch wide **GREEN/BEIGE PLAID** side outer border strips to this length. Sew the 3-1/2-inch **GREEN** corner squares to both ends of the border strips; press. Sew the strips to the side edges of the quilt center.

Putting It All Together

Cut the 3 yard length of backing fabric in half crosswise to make 2, 1-1/2 yard lengths.
Refer to **Finishing the Quilt** on page 215 for complete instructions.

Binding

Cutting

From **GREEN PRINT:**
- Cut 6, 2-3/4 x 42-inch strips

Sew the binding to the quilt using a 3/8-inch seam allowance. This measurement will produce a 1/2-inch wide finished double binding. Refer to **Binding and Diagonal Piecing** instructions on page 215.

Oh Baby, Baby

47 x 55-inches

Sweet Retreat

Pink

Soft as a butterfly wing, Flying Geese
blocks take flight in a muted palette
of pink, beige, and soft green. A limited
number of fabrics and large pieces make
this a perfect weekend patchwork project.

Sweet Retreat
Pink

72-inches square

Fabrics & Supplies

1-1/8 yards **PINK PRINT** for blocks

2-1/4 yards **BEIGE PRINT**
for blocks and borders

1-1/8 yards **GREEN FLORAL** for blocks

2 yards **LARGE BEIGE FLORAL**
for blocks and outer border

1-3/4 yards **GREEN PRINT**
for blocks and borders

5/8 yard **SMALL BEIGE FLORAL** for blocks

1 yard **GREEN PLAID**
for binding (cut on the bias)

4-1/2 yards backing fabric

quilt batting, at least 78-inches square

Before beginning this project,
read through **Getting Started** on page 210.

Block A

Makes 5 blocks

Cutting

From **PINK PRINT:**
- Cut 7, 2-1/2 x 42-inch strips. From the strips cut:
  60, 2-1/2 x 4-1/2-inch rectangles

From **BEIGE PRINT:**
- Cut 8, 2-1/2 x 42-inch strips. From the strips cut:
  120, 2-1/2-inch squares

From **GREEN FLORAL:**
- Cut 2, 6-7/8 x 42-inch strips
- Cut 1, 4-1/2 x 42-inch strip. From the strip cut:
  5, 4-1/2-inch squares

From **LARGE BEIGE FLORAL:**
- Cut 2, 6-7/8 x 42-inch strips

Piecing

Step 1   With right sides together, position a
2-1/2-inch **BEIGE** square on the corner of a
2-1/2 x 4-1/2-inch **PINK** rectangle. Draw a diagonal
line on the square and stitch on the line. Trim the
seam allowance to 1/4-inch; press. Repeat this process
at the opposite corner of the rectangle.

Make 60 flying geese units

Step 2   Sew together 3 of the Step 1 units; press.
At this point each flying geese unit should measure
4-1/2 x 6-1/2-inches.

Make 20

Step 3   Sew a flying geese unit to both side edges of
a 4-1/2-inch **GREEN FLORAL** square; press.

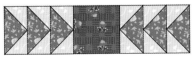

Make 5

78

Step 4 With right sides together, layer together the 6-7/8 x 42-inch **LARGE BEIGE FLORAL** and **GREEN FLORAL** strips in pairs. Press together, but do not sew. Cut the layered strips into squares. Cut each layered square in half diagonally to make 20 sets of triangles. Stitch 1/4-inch from the diagonal edge of each pair of triangles; press.

Crosscut 10, 6-7/8-inch squares

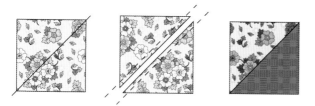

Make 20, 6-1/2-inch triangle-pieced squares

Step 5 Sew a triangle-pieced square to both side edges of a flying geese unit; press.

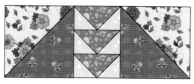

Make 10

Step 6 Referring to the block diagram, sew Step 5 units to both side edges of a Step 3 unit; press. At this point each block should measure 16-1/2-inches square.

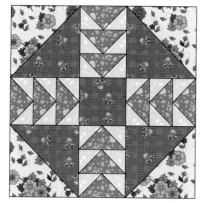

Block A, Make 5

Block B

Makes 4 blocks

Cutting

Note: *You may need to cut an extra strip from each of these fabrics.*

From **PINK PRINT:**
- Cut 2, 5-1/4 x 42-inch strips. From the strips cut: 16, 5-1/4-inch squares. Cut the squares diagonally into quarters to make 64 triangles.

From **GREEN PRINT:**
- Cut 2, 5-1/4 x 42-inch strips. From the strips cut: 16, 5-1/4-inch squares. Cut the squares diagonally into quarters to make 64 triangles.

From **SMALL BEIGE FLORAL:**
- Cut 3, 5-1/4 x 42-inch strips. From the strips cut: 16, 5-1/4-inch squares. Cut the squares diagonally into quarters to make 64 triangles.

From **GREEN FLORAL:**
- Cut 3, 5-1/4 x 42-inch strips. From the strips cut: 16, 5-1/4-inch squares. Cut the squares diagonally into quarters to make 64 triangles.

Piecing

Step 1 With right sides together, layer the **PINK** and **GREEN PRINT** triangles in pairs. Stitch along the same bias edge of each pair of triangles being careful not to stretch the triangles; press. Sew the triangle units together in pairs; press. At this point each hourglass unit should measure 4-1/2-inches square.

Bias edges

Make 64 triangle units   Make 32 hourglass units

Step 2   With right sides together, layer the **SMALL BEIGE FLORAL** and **GREEN FLORAL** triangles in pairs. Stitch along the bias edge; press. Sew the triangle units together in pairs; press. <u>At this point each hourglass unit should measure 4-1/2-inches square.</u>

Bias edges

Make 64
triangle units

Make 32
hourglass units

Step 3   Referring to the block diagram, sew together the Step 1 and Step 2 hourglass units in 4 rows of 4 hourglass units each. Press the seam allowances in alternating directions by rows so the seams will fit snugly together with less bulk. Sew the rows together; press. <u>At this point each block should measure 16-1/2-inches square.</u>

Block B, Make 4

Quilt Center

Step 1   Referring to the quilt diagram for block placement, sew together the **A** and **B Blocks** in 3 rows of 3 blocks each. Press the seam allowances toward the **A Blocks** so the seams will fit snugly together with less bulk.

Step 2   Pin the rows together at the block intersections; sew the rows together and press. <u>At this point the quilt center should measure 48-1/2-inches square.</u>

Borders

*Note: The yardage given allows for the border strips to be cut on the crosswise grain. Diagonally piece the strips as needed, referring to **Diagonal Piecing** instructions on page 215. Read through **Border** instructions on page 214 for general instructions on adding borders.*

Cutting

From **BEIGE PRINT**:
- Cut 12, 1-1/2 x 42-inch border strips
- Cut 14, 2-1/2 x 42-inch strips.
    From the strips cut:
    216, 2-1/2-inch squares for flying geese

From **GREEN PRINT**:
- Cut 6, 1 x 42-inch middle border strips
- Cut 13, 2-1/2 x 42-inch strips.
    From the strips cut:
    108, 2-1/2 x 4-1/2-inch rectangles for flying geese

From **LARGE BEIGE FLORAL**:
- Cut 8, 6 x 42-inch outer border strips

Attaching the Borders

Step 1   Attach the first 1-1/2-inch wide **BEIGE** border strips.

Step 2   With right sides together, position a 2-1/2-inch **BEIGE** square on the corner of a 2-1/2 x 4-1/2-inch **GREEN** rectangle. Draw a diagonal line on the square; stitch, trim, and press. Repeat this process at the opposite corner of the rectangle.

Make 108 flying geese units

Step 3   Sew 25 flying geese units together for the top/bottom borders; press. Sew the border strips to the top/bottom edges of the quilt; press.

Step 4   Sew 29 flying geese units together for the side borders; press. Sew the border strips to the side edges of the quilt; press.

Step 5 Attach the second 1-1/2-inch wide **BEIGE** border strips.

Step 6 Attach the 1-inch wide **GREEN** border strips.

Step 7 Attach the 6-inch wide **LARGE BEIGE FLORAL** border strips.

Putting It All Together

Cut the 4-1/2 yard length of backing fabric in half crosswise to make 2, 2-1/4 yard lengths. Refer to **Finishing the Quilt** on page 215 for complete instructions.

Binding

Cutting

From **GREEN PLAID**:
• Cut enough 2-3/4-inch wide **bias** strips to make a 300-inch long strip.

Sew the binding to the quilt using a 3/8-inch seam allowance. This measurement will produce a 1/2-inch wide finished double binding. Refer to **Binding and Diagonal Piecing** on page 215 for complete instructions.

Sweet Retreat
Pink

72-inches square

Sweet Retreat

Plaid

72-inches square

Fabrics & Supplies

1-1/8 yards **RED PLAID** for blocks

2-1/4 yards **BEIGE PRINT**
for blocks and borders

1-1/8 yards **GREEN PLAID** for blocks

2 yards **LARGE TAN FLORAL**
for blocks and outer border

1-3/4 yards **BLACK PLAID**
for blocks and borders

5/8 yard **TAN PLAID** for blocks

1 yard **BLACK PLAID**
for binding (cut on the bias)

4-1/2 yards backing fabric

quilt batting, at least 78-inches square

Before beginning this project,
read through **Getting Started** on page 210.

Block A

Makes 5 blocks

Cutting

From **RED PLAID**:
• Cut 7, 2-1/2 x 42-inch strips. From the strips cut:
  60, 2-1/2 x 4-1/2-inch rectangles

From **BEIGE PRINT**:
• Cut 8, 2-1/2 x 42-inch strips. From the strips cut:
  120, 2-1/2-inch squares

From **GREEN PLAID**:
• Cut 2, 6-7/8 x 42-inch strips
• Cut 1, 4-1/2 x 42-inch strip. From the strip cut:
  5, 4-1/2-inch squares

From **LARGE TAN FLORAL**:
• Cut 2, 6-7/8 x 42-inch strips

Piecing

Step 1 With right sides together, position a
2-1/2-inch **BEIGE** square on the corner of a
2-1/2 x 4-1/2-inch **RED PLAID** rectangle. Draw a
diagonal line on the square and stitch on the line.
Trim the seam allowance to 1/4-inch; press. Repeat
this process at the opposite corner of the rectangle.

Make 60 flying geese units

Step 2   Sew together 3 of the Step 1 units; press. <u>At this point each flying geese unit should measure 4-1/2 x 6-1/2-inches.</u>

Make 20

Step 3   Sew a flying geese unit to both side edges of a 4-1/2-inch **GREEN PLAID** square; press.

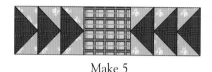

Make 5

Step 4   With right sides together, layer together the 6-7/8 x 42-inch **LARGE TAN FLORAL** and **GREEN PLAID** strips in pairs. Press together, but do not sew. Cut the layered strips into squares. Cut each layered square in half diagonally to make 20 sets of triangles. Stitch 1/4-inch from the diagonal edge of each pair of triangles; press.

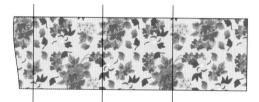

Crosscut 10, 6-7/8-inch squares

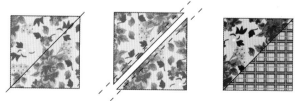

Make 20, 6-1/2-inch triangle-pieced squares

Step 5   Sew a triangle-pieced square to both side edges of a flying geese unit; press.

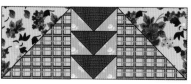

Make 10

Step 6   Referring to the block diagram, sew Step 5 units to both side edges of a Step 3 unit; press. <u>At this point each block should measure 16-1/2-inches square.</u>

Block A, Make 5

Block B

Makes 4 blocks

Cutting

Note: You may need to cut an extra strip from each of these fabrics.

From **RED PLAID:**
- Cut 2, 5-1/4 x 42-inch strips. From the strips cut: 16, 5-1/4-inch squares. Cut the squares diagonally into quarters to make 64 triangles.

From **BLACK PLAID:**
- Cut 2, 5-1/4 x 42-inch strips. From the strips cut: 16, 5-1/4-inch squares. Cut the squares diagonally into quarters to make 64 triangles.

From **TAN PLAID:**
- Cut 3, 5-1/4 x 42-inch strips. From the strips cut: 16, 5-1/4-inch squares. Cut the squares diagonally into quarters to make 64 triangles.

From **GREEN PLAID:**
- Cut 3, 5-1/4 x 42-inch strips. From the strips cut: 16, 5-1/4-inch squares. Cut the squares diagonally into quarters to make 64 triangles.

Piecing

Step 1   With right sides together, layer the **RED PLAID** and **BLACK PLAID** triangles in pairs. Stitch along the same bias edge of each pair of triangles being careful not to stretch the triangles; press. Sew the triangle units together in pairs; press. At this point each hourglass unit should measure 4-1/2-inches square.

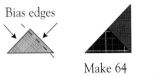

Make 64 triangle units   Make 32 hourglass blocks

Step 2 With right sides together, layer the **TAN PLAID** and **GREEN PLAID** triangles in pairs. Stitch along the bias edge; press. Sew the triangle units together in pairs; press. At this point each hourglass unit should measure 4-1/2-inches square.

Make 64 triangle units   Make 32 hourglass blocks

Step 3 Referring to the block diagram, sew together the Step 1 and Step 2 hourglass units in 4 rows of 4 hourglass units each. Press the seam allowances in alternating directions by rows so the seams will fit snugly together with less bulk. Sew the rows together; press. At this point each block should measure 16-1/2-inches square.

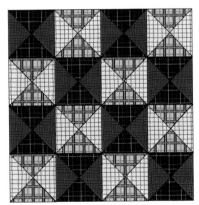

Block B, Make 4

Quilt Center

Step 1 Referring to the quilt diagram for block placement, sew together the **A** and **B Blocks** in 3 rows of 3 blocks each. Press the seam allowances toward the **A Blocks** so the seams will fit snugly together with less bulk.

Step 2 Pin the rows together at the block intersections; sew the rows together and press. At this point the quilt center should measure 48-1/2-inches square.

Borders

Note: *The yardage given allows for the border strips to be cut on the crosswise grain. Diagonally piece the strips as needed, referring to **Diagonal Piecing** instructions on page 215. Read through **Border** instructions on page 214 for general instructions on adding borders.*

Cutting

From **BEIGE PRINT**:
- Cut 12, 1-1/2 x 42-inch border strips
- Cut 14, 2-1/2 x 42-inch strips.
    From the strips cut:
    216, 2-1/2-inch squares for flying geese

From **BLACK PLAID**:
- Cut 6, 1 x 42-inch middle border strips
- Cut 13, 2-1/2 x 42-inch strips.
    From the strips cut:
    108, 2-1/2 x 4-1/2-inch rectangles for flying geese

From **LARGE TAN FLORAL**:
- Cut 8, 6 x 42-inch outer border strips

Attaching the Borders

Step 1 Attach the first 1-1/2-inch wide **BEIGE** border strips.

Step 2 With right sides together, position a 2-1/2-inch **BEIGE** square on the corner of a 2-1/2 x 4-1/2-inch **BLACK PLAID** rectangle. Draw a diagonal line on the square; stitch, trim, and press. Repeat this process at the opposite corner of the rectangle.

Make 108 flying geese units

Step 3 Sew 25 flying geese units together for the top/bottom borders; press. Sew the border strips to the top/bottom edges of the quilt; press.

Step 4 Sew 29 flying geese units together for the side borders; press. Sew the border strips to the side edges of the quilt; press.

Step 5 Attach the second 1-1/2-inch wide **BEIGE** border strips.

Step 6 Attach the 1-inch wide **BLACK PLAID** border strips.

Step 7 Attach the 6-inch wide **LARGE TAN FLORAL** border strips.

Putting It All Together

Cut the 4-1/2 yard length of backing fabric in half crosswise to make 2, 2-1/4 yard lengths.

Refer to **Finishing the Quilt** on page 215 for complete instructions.

Binding

Cutting

From **BLACK PLAID:**
• Cut enough 2-3/4-inch wide **bias** strips to make a 300-inch long strip.

Sew the binding to the quilt using a 3/8-inch seam allowance. This measurement will produce a 1/2-inch wide finished double binding. Refer to **Binding and Diagonal Piecing** on page 215 for complete instructions.

Sweet Retreat Plaid

72-inches square

Mountain Stars

Catch a falling star and put it on your wall! In a dazzling display of design inspiration, half-square triangles and Hourglass blocks twist, turn, combine—and combine again to create this star-studded beauty.

Mountain Stars

76 x 92-inches

Fabrics & Supplies

1-1/3 yards **GOLD PRINT #1**
for star block points and point rows

2/3 yard **GOLD PRINT #2**
for star block centers and corner squares

2-5/8 yards **BEIGE PRINT** for background

1-7/8 yards **BLACK PRINT** for point rows, inner
border, middle border, and pieced border

3-1/4 yards **RED PRINT #1** for point rows,
hourglass blocks, pieced border, and outer border

1-1/8 yards **RED PRINT #2** for middle border

7/8 yard **BLACK PLAID**
for binding (cut on the bias)

5-1/2 yards backing fabric

quilt batting, at least 82 x 98-inches

Before beginning this project,
read through **Getting Started** on page 210.

Star Blocks

Makes 27 blocks

Cutting

From **GOLD PRINT #1:**
- Cut 14, 2-1/2 x 42-inch strips. From the strips cut:
  216, 2-1/2-inch squares

From **GOLD PRINT #2:**
- Cut 3, 4-1/2 x 42-inch strips. From the strips cut:
  27, 4-1/2-inch squares for star blocks and
  corner squares

From **BEIGE PRINT:**
- Cut 19, 2-1/2 x 42-inch strips. From the strips cut:
  108, 2-1/2 x 4-1/2-inch rectangles
  108, 2-1/2-inch squares

Piecing

Step 1   Position a 2-1/2-inch **GOLD PRINT #1**
square on the corner of a 2-1/2 x 4-1/2-inch **BEIGE**
rectangle. Draw a diagonal line on the square and
stitch on the line. Trim the seam allowance to
1/4-inch; press. Repeat this process at the opposite
corner of the rectangle.

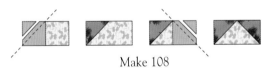

Make 108

Step 2   Sew Step 1 star point units to the
top/bottom edges of the 4-1/2-inch **GOLD PRINT
#2** squares; press. Sew 2-1/2-inch **BEIGE** squares to
both ends of the remaining Step 1 star point units;
press. Sew the units to both side edges of the **GOLD**
square units; press.

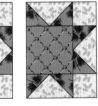

Make 27

Step 3   Referring to the quilt diagram, sew 3 star
blocks together for the quilt center; press. Set the
remaining star blocks aside to be used later.

Point Rows

Cutting

From BLACK PRINT:
- Cut 2, 2-1/2 x 42-inch strips. From the strips cut:
  - 4, 2-1/2 x 4-1/2-inch rectangles
  - 16, 2-1/2-inch squares
- Cut 1, 2-7/8 x 42-inch strip

From RED PRINT #1:
- Cut 2, 2-1/2 x 42-inch strips. From the strips cut:
  - 4, 2-1/2 x 4-1/2-inch rectangles
  - 16, 2-1/2-inch squares
- Cut 1, 2-7/8 x 42-inch strip

From GOLD PRINT #1:
- Cut 2, 2-1/2 x 42-inch strips. From the strips cut:
  - 4, 2-1/2 x 4-1/2-inch rectangles
  - 16, 2-1/2-inch squares
- Cut 1, 2-7/8 x 42-inch strip

From BEIGE PRINT:
- Cut 5, 2-1/2 x 42-inch strips. From the strips cut:
  - 24, 2-1/2 x 4-1/2-inch rectangles
  - 28, 2-1/2-inch squares
- Cut 3, 2-7/8 x 42-inch strips

From GOLD PRINT #2:
- Cut 1, 4-1/2 x 42-inch strip. From the strip cut:
  - 4, 4-1/2-inch corner squares

Piecing

Step 1 Position a 2-1/2-inch **BLACK** square on the corner of a 2-1/2 x 4-1/2-inch **BEIGE** rectangle. Draw a diagonal line on the square; stitch, trim, and press. Repeat this process at the opposite corner of the rectangle.

Make 8

Step 2 Repeat Step 1 using 2-1/2-inch **RED #1** squares and 2-1/2 x 4-1/2-inch **BEIGE** rectangles. Make 8 units. Repeat this process using 2-1/2-inch **GOLD #1** squares and 2-1/2 x 4-1/2-inch **BEIGE** rectangles. Make 8 units.

Make 8   Make 8

Step 3 Position a 2-1/2-inch **BEIGE** square on the corner of a 2-1/2 x 4-1/2-inch **BLACK** rectangle. Draw a diagonal line on the square; stitch, trim, and press. Repeat this process at the opposite corner of the rectangle.

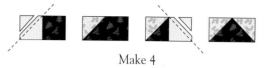

Make 4

Step 4 Repeat Step 3 using 2-1/2-inch **BEIGE** squares and 2-1/2 x 4-1/2-inch **RED #1** rectangles. Make 4 units. Repeat this process using 2-1/2-inch **BEIGE** squares and 2-1/2 x 4-1/2-inch **GOLD #1** rectangles. Make 4 units.

Make 4   Make 4

Step 5 With right sides together, layer a 2-7/8 x 42-inch **BLACK** and **BEIGE** strip. Press together, but do not sew. Cut the layered strip into squares. Cut each layered square in half diagonally to make 8 sets of triangles. Stitch 1/4-inch from the diagonal edge of each pair of triangles; press.

Crosscut 4,   Make 8, 2-1/2-inch
2-7/8-inch squares   triangled-pieced squares

Step 6 Repeat Step 5 using a 2-7/8 x 42-inch **RED #1** and **BEIGE** strip. Cut the layered strip into 8, 2-7/8-inch squares to make 16, 2-1/2-inch triangle-pieced squares. Repeat this process using a 2-7/8 x 42-inch **GOLD #1** strip and **BEIGE** strip. Cut the layered strip into 8, 2-7/8-inch squares to make 16, 2-1/2-inch triangle-pieced squares.

Make 16, 2-1/2-inch triangled-pieced squares

Make 16, 2-1/2-inch triangled-pieced squares

Step 7 For the top/bottom **BLACK/BEIGE** point rows, sew a Step 5 triangle-pieced square to both sides of a Step 1 unit; press. Make 2 point rows. Sew the point rows to the top/bottom edges of the star block quilt center; press.

Make 2

Step 8 For the side **BLACK/BEIGE** point rows, sew together 2 of the Step 5 triangle-pieced squares, 3 of the Step 1 units, 2 of the Step 3 **BLACK/BEIGE** units, and 2 of the 2-1/2-inch **BEIGE** squares; press. Make 2 point rows. Sew the point rows to the side edges of the star block quilt center; press.

Make 2

Step 9 For the top/bottom **RED/BEIGE** point rows, sew 2 of the Step 6 **RED/BEIGE** triangle-pieced squares to both side edges of a Step 2 **RED/BEIGE** unit; press.

Make 2

Step 10 For the top/bottom **GOLD/BEIGE** point rows, repeat the process in Step 9 using the Step 6 **GOLD/BEIGE** triangle-pieced squares and the Step 2 **GOLD/BEIGE** units; press. Make 2 point rows. Sew the **GOLD/BEIGE** point rows to the top edge of the Step 9 **RED/BEIGE** point rows; press. Make 2 units. Sew the units to the top/bottom edges of the star block quilt center; press.

Make 2

Make 2

Step 11 For the side **RED/BEIGE** point rows, sew together the remaining **RED/BEIGE** triangle-pieced squares, and the **RED/BEIGE** Step 2 and Step 4 units as diagramed; press.

Make 2

Step 12 For the side **GOLD/BEIGE** point rows, sew together the remaining **GOLD/BEIGE** triangle-pieced squares, and the **GOLD/BEIGE** Step 2 and Step 4 units as diagramed; press.

Make 2

Step 13 Sew the Step 11 **RED/BEIGE** strips to the bottom edge of the Step 12 **GOLD/BEIGE** strips; press. Sew the 4-1/2-inch **GOLD PRINT #2** corner squares to both ends of the side strips; press. Referring to the quilt center assembly diagram, sew the point rows to the quilt; press. At this point the quilt center should measure 20-1/2 x 36-1/2-inches.

Quilt Center Assembly

Hourglass Blocks

Makes 32 blocks

Cutting

From **RED PRINT #1:**
- Cut 3, 5-1/4 x 42-inch strips. From the strips cut: 16, 5-1/4-inch squares. Cut the squares diagonally into quarters to make 64 triangles.

From **BEIGE PRINT:**
- Cut 3, 5-1/4 x 42-inch strips. From the strips cut: 16, 5-1/4-inch squares. Cut the squares diagonally into quarters to make 64 triangles.

Piecing

Step 1   With right sides together, layer the **BEIGE** and **RED** triangles together in pairs. Stitch along the same bias edge of each pair of triangles being careful not to stretch the triangles; press. Sew the triangle units together in pairs; press. <u>At this point each hourglass block should measure 4-1/2-inches square.</u>

 Bias edges

Make 64 triangle units   Make 32

Step 2   For the top/bottom hourglass block borders, sew together 5 hourglass blocks; press. Make 2 borders. <u>At this point each hourglass block border should measure 4-1/2 x 20-1/2-inches.</u> Sew the borders to the top/bottom edges of the quilt center; press.

Make 2

Step 3   For the side hourglass block borders, sew together 11 hourglass blocks; press. Make 2 borders. <u>At this point each hourglass block border should measure 4-1/2 x 44-1/2-inches.</u> Sew the borders to the side edges of the quilt center; press.

Make 2

Borders

Note: *The yardage given allows for the border strips to be cut on the crosswise grain. Diagonally piece the strips as needed, referring to **Diagonal Piecing** instructions on page 215. Read through **Border** instructions on page 214 for general instructions on adding borders.*

Cutting

From **BLACK PRINT:**
- Cut 5, 2-1/2 x 42-inch inner border strips
- Cut 7 more 2-1/2 x 42-inch narrow middle border strips
- Cut 8 more 2-1/2 x 42-inch strips. From the strips cut: 68, 2-1/2 x 4-1/2-inch rectangles for pieced border

From **RED PRINT #2:**
- Cut 7, 4-1/2 x 42-inch wide middle border strips

From **RED PRINT #1:**
- Cut 9, 2-1/2 x 42-inch strips. From the strips cut: 140, 2-1/2-inch squares for pieced border
- Cut 9, 6-1/2 x 42-inch outer border strips

Attaching the Borders

Refer to the Quilt Assembly Diagram on page 92 for placement.

Step 1   Attach the 2-1/2-inch wide **BLACK** inner border strips.

Step 2   For the top/bottom star block borders, sew together 4 star blocks; press. Sew the borders to the top/bottom edges of the quilt center; press. For the side star block borders, sew together 8 star blocks; press. Sew the borders to the side edges of the quilt center; press. <u>At this point the quilt center should measure 48-1/2 x 64-1/2-inches.</u>

Step 3   Attach the 2-1/2-inch wide **BLACK** narrow middle border strips.

Step 4   Attach the 4-1/2-inch wide **RED PRINT #2** wide middle border strips.

Step 5   To make the units for the pieced border, position a 2-1/2-inch **RED PRINT #1** square on the corner of a 2-1/2 x 4-1/2-inch **BLACK** rectangle. Draw a diagonal line on the square; stitch, trim, and press. Repeat this process at the opposite corner of the rectangle.

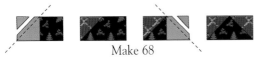

Make 68

Step 6   For the top/bottom pieced borders, sew together 15 of the Step 5 units; press. Sew the borders to the top/bottom edges of the quilt; press. For the side pieced borders, sew together 19 of the Step 5 units; press. Sew 2-1/2-inch **RED PRINT #1** corner squares to both ends of the strips; press. Sew the borders to the side edges of the quilt; press. At this point the quilt center should measure 64-1/2 x 80-1/2-inches.

Step 7   Attach the 6-1/2-inch wide **RED PRINT #1** outer border strips.

Quilt Assembly Diagram

Putting It All Together

Cut the 5-1/2-yard length of backing fabric in half crosswise to make 2, 2-3/4 yard lengths. Refer to **Finishing the Quilt** on page 215 for complete instructions.

Binding

Cutting

From **BLACK PLAID:**
- Cut enough 2-3/4-inch wide **bias** strips to make a 350-inch long strip.

Sew the binding to the quilt using a 3/8-inch seam allowance. This measurement will produce a 1/2-inch wide finished double binding. Refer to **Binding and Diagonal Piecing** instructions on page 215 for complete instructions.

Mountain Stars

76 x 92-inches

Up North

Dreaming of a small cabin up north surrounded by towering pine trees? Now you can have it all right in your own home. Tall timbers, eight-pointed stars and big blocks are all a part of this easy, easy and oh, so very cozy flannel quilt.

72 x 90-inches

Fabrics & Supplies

1-1/4 yards **GREEN PRINT** for trees

1 yard **BEIGE PRINT** for tree background

3/4 yard **BROWN DIAGONAL PRINT**
for tree trunks and inner border

7/8 yard **CHESTNUT TICKING**
for horizontal rectangles and middle border

1/2 yard **GOLD PRINT** for stars

1/2 yard **CREAM PRINT** for star background

1/4 yard *each* of **11 DARK PRINTS**
for vertical strips

2-3/4 yards **GREEN FLORAL** for outer border

7/8 yard **BROWN DIAGONAL PRINT**
for binding

5-1/3 yards backing fabric

quilt batting, at least 78 x 96-inches

Before beginning this project,
read through **Getting Started** on page 210.

Tree Blocks

Makes 9 blocks

Cutting

From **GREEN PRINT**:
- Cut 3, 4-1/2 x 42-inch strips. From the strips cut:
  9, 4-1/2 x 8-1/2-inch rectangles
- Cut 9, 2-1/2 x 42-inch strips. From the strips cut:
  32, 2-1/2 x 8-1/2-inch rectangles

From **BEIGE PRINT**:
- Cut 2, 4-1/2 x 42-inch strips. From the strips cut:
  18, 4-1/2-inch squares
- Cut 4, 2-1/2 x 42-inch strips. From the strips cut:
  64, 2-1/2-inch squares
- Cut 2, 3-1/2 x 42-inch strips

From **BROWN DIAGONAL PRINT**:
- Cut 1, 2-1/2 x 42-inch strip

From **CHESTNUT TICKING**:
- Cut 2, 2-1/2 x 42-inch strips. From the strips cut:
  7, 2-1/2 x 8-1/2-inch rectangles

Piecing

Step 1 With right sides together, position a
4-1/2-inch **BEIGE** square on the corner of a
4-1/2 x 8-1/2-inch **GREEN** rectangle. Draw a
diagonal line on the square and stitch on the
line. Trim the seam allowance to 1/4-inch; press.
Repeat this process at the opposite corner of the
rectangle; press.

Make 9 tree top units

Step 2 With right sides together, position
2-1/2-inch **BEIGE** squares on the corners
of a 2-1/2 x 8-1/2-inch **GREEN** rectangle. Draw a
diagonal line on the squares; stitch, trim, and press.

Make 32

Step 3 Sew a 3-1/2 x 42-inch **BEIGE** strip to both side edges of the 2-1/2 x 42-inch **BROWN DIAGONAL PRINT** strip; press. Cut the strip set into segments.

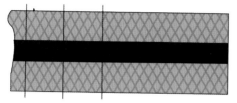

Crosscut 9, 4-1/2-inch wide segments for tree trunk units

Step 4 To assemble the tall trees, sew 4 of the Step 2 units together, and sew a Step 1 tree top unit to the top edge. Sew a Step 3 tree trunk unit to the bottom edge of the unit; press. Make 5 tall trees. At this point each tall tree should measure 8-1/2 x 16-1/2-inches. **Note:** Referring to the quilt diagram, sew a 2-1/2 x 8-1/2-inch **CHESTNUT TICKING** rectangle to the bottom edge of 3 of the tall tree blocks; press. At this point 3 of the tall trees should measure 8-1/2 x 18-1/2-inches.

Make 5 tall trees

Step 5 To assemble the short trees, sew 3 of the Step 2 units together, and sew a Step 1 tree top unit to the top edge. Sew a Step 3 tree trunk unit to the bottom edge of the unit; press. Make 4 short trees. Sew 2-1/2 x 8-1/2-inch **CHESTNUT TICKING** rectangles to the bottom edge of the tree blocks; press. At this point each short tree should measure 8-1/2 x 16-1/2-inches.

Make 4 short trees

Star Blocks

Makes 6 blocks

Cutting

From **GOLD PRINT:**
- Cut 1, 4-1/2 x 42-inch strip. From the strip cut: 6, 4-1/2-inch squares
- Cut 3, 2-1/2 x 42-inch strips. From the strips cut: 48, 2-1/2-inch squares

From **CREAM PRINT:**
- Cut 5, 2-1/2 x 42-inch strips. From the strips cut: 24, 2-1/2 x 4-1/2-inch rectangles 24, 2-1/2-inch squares

Piecing

Step 1 Position a 2-1/2-inch **GOLD** square at the corner of a 2-1/2 x 4-1/2-inch **CREAM** rectangle. Draw a diagonal line on the square; stitch, trim, and press. Repeat this process at the opposite corner of the rectangle; press.

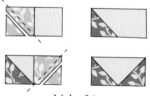

Make 24

Step 2 Sew Step 1 star point units to the top/bottom edges of the 4-1/2-inch **GOLD** square; press. Sew 2-1/2-inch **CREAM** squares to both ends of the remaining star point units; press. Sew the units to the side edges of the square unit; press. At this point each star block should measure 8-1/2-inches square.

Make 6   Make 6

Quilt Center

Cutting

From *each* of the **11 DARK PRINTS**:
- Cut 1, 6-1/2 x 42-inch strip.
    From *each* of the strips cut:
    4, 6-1/2-inch squares

Piecing

Step 1   Referring to the quilt diagram for placement, sew the tree blocks and the star blocks together in 3 vertical rows; press.

Step 2   Referring to the quilt diagram for color placement, sew the 6-1/2-inch **DARK PRINT** squares together in 4 vertical rows of 11 squares each; press.

Step 3   Sew the Step 1 and Step 2 rows together; press.

Borders

Note: *The yardage given allows for the border strips to be cut on the crosswise grain. Diagonally piece the strips as needed, referring to* **Diagonal Piecing** *instructions on page 215. Read through* **Border** *instructions on page 214 for general instructions on adding borders.*

Cutting

From **BROWN DIAGONAL PRINT:**
- Cut 7, 2-1/2 x 42-inch inner border strips

From **CHESTNUT TICKING:**
- Cut 7, 2-1/2 x 42-inch middle border strips

From **GREEN FLORAL:**
- Cut 10, 8-1/2 x 42-inch outer border strips

Attaching the Borders

Step 1   Attach the 2-1/2-inch wide **BROWN DIAGONAL PRINT** inner border strips.

Step 2   Attach the 2-1/2-inch wide **CHESTNUT TICKING** middle border strips.

Step 3   Attach the 8-1/2-inch **GREEN FLORAL** outer border strips.

Putting It All Together

Cut the 5-1/3 yard length of backing fabric in half crosswise to make 2, 2-2/3 yard lengths. Refer to **Finishing the Quilt** on page 215 for complete instructions.

Binding

Cutting

From **BROWN DIAGONAL PRINT:**
- Cut 9, 2-3/4 x 42-inch strips

Sew the binding to the quilt using a 3/8-inch seam allowance. This measurement will produce a 1/2-inch wide finished double binding. Refer to **Binding and Diagonal Piecing** on page 215 for complete instructions.

Up North
72 x 90-inches

Hourglass Patches

Reminiscent of an English cottage
garden, a cascade of floral print
blossoms enhances the simple
sophistication of the Hourglass patches.

Hourglass Patches

70 x 76-inches

Fabrics & Supplies

2 yards **GREEN FLORAL** for hourglass blocks, alternate blocks, and corner squares

1-3/4 yards **BEIGE PRINT** for hourglass blocks and alternate blocks

1/2 yard **BLUE PRINT** for inner border

2 yards **GREEN STRIP** for outer border

3/4 yard **GREEN PLAID** for binding (cut on the bias)

4-2/3 yards backing fabric

quilt batting, at least 76 x 82-inches

Before beginning this project, read through **Getting Started** on page 210.

Hourglass Blocks

Makes 28 blocks

Cutting

From **GREEN FLORAL:**
• Cut 4, 9-1/4 x 42-inch strips. From the strips cut: 14, 9-1/4-inch squares

From **BEIGE PRINT:**
• Cut 4, 9-1/4 x 42-inch strips. From the strips cut: 14, 9-1/4-inch squares

Piecing

To make the hourglass blocks, with right sides together, layer the 9-1/4-inch **GREEN FLORAL** and **BEIGE** squares in pairs. Press together, but do not sew. Cut the layered squares diagonally into quarters to make 56 sets of triangles. Stitch along the same bias edge of each pair of triangles being careful not to stretch the triangles; press. Sew the triangle units together in pairs to make the hourglass blocks; press. <u>At this point each hourglass block should measure 8-1/2-inches square.</u>

Bias edges

Make 56 triangle units   Make 28 hourglass blocks

Quilt Center

Cutting

From **GREEN FLORAL:**
• Cut 3, 6-1/2 x 42-inch strips. From the strips cut: 12, 6-1/2 x 8-1/2-inch rectangles

From **BEIGE PRINT:**
• Cut 3, 6-1/2 x 42-inch strips. From the strips cut: 9, 6-1/2 x 8-1/2-inch rectangles

Quilt Center Assembly

Step 1 Sew together 4 of the hourglass blocks and 3 of the 6-1/2 x 8-1/2-inch **GREEN FLORAL** alternate blocks. Press the seam allowances toward the alternate blocks. Make 4 blocks rows. <u>At this point each block row should measure 8-1/2 x 50-1/2-inches.</u>

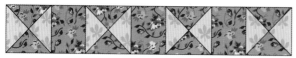

Make 4 block rows

Step 2   Sew together 4 of the hourglass blocks and 3 of the 6-1/2 x 8-1/2-inch **BEIGE** alternate blocks. Press the seam allowances toward the hourglass blocks. Make 3 block rows. <u>At this point each block row should measure 8-1/2 x 50-1/2-inches.</u>

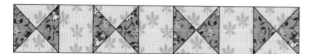

Make 3 block rows

Step 3   Referring to the quilt diagram for placement, pin the block rows together at the block intersections and sew them together; press. <u>At this point the quilt center should measure 50-1/2 x 56-1/2-inches.</u>

Borders

Note: *The yardage given allows for the border strips to be cut on the crosswise grain. Diagonally piece the strips as needed, referring to* **Diagonal Piecing** *instructions on page 215. Read through* **Border** *instructions on page 214 for general instructions on adding borders.*

Cutting

From **BLUE PRINT:**
• Cut 6, 2-1/2 x 42-inch inner border strips

From **GREEN STRIPE:**
• Cut 8, 8-1/2 x 42-inch outer border strips

From **GREEN FLORAL:**
• Cut 1, 8-1/2 x 42-inch strip. From the strip cut: 4, 8-1/2-inch corner squares

Attaching the Borders

Step 1   Attach the 2-1/2-inch wide **BLUE** inner border strips.

Step 2   Attach the 8-1/2-inch wide **GREEN STRIPE** top/bottom outer border strips. For the side outer border, measure the quilt including the seam allowances, but not the top/bottom borders just added. Cut the 8-1/2-inch wide **GREEN STRIPE** side outer border strips to this length.

Sew 8-1/2-inch **GREEN FLORAL** corner squares to both ends of the **GREEN STRIPE** side border strips. Sew the border strips to the side edges of the quilt center.

Putting It All Together

Cut the 4-2/3 yard length of backing fabric in half crosswise to make 2, 2-1/3 yard lengths. Refer to **Finishing the Quilt** on page 215 for complete instructions.

Binding

Cutting

From **GREEN PLAID:**
• Cut enough 2-3/4-inch wide strips to make a 300-inch long strip.

Sew the binding to the quilt using a 3/8-inch seam allowance. This measurement will produce a 1/2-inch wide finished double binding. Refer to **Binding and Diagonal Piecing** on page 215 for complete instructions.

Hourglass Patches

70 x 76-inches

Winter Memories

Thoughts of wintertime fun almost always
bring back warm memories of mittens
made by hand with love. Hand-knitted
mittens embellished with vintage buttons
stay handy in an old wooden box painted
red and stenciled with mittens, snowflakes,
and stars to complement the tonal stars
and Log Cabin blocks which form the
backdrop for whimsical appliqués.

Winter Memories

64 x 72-inches

Fabrics & Supplies

1-1/3 yards **LIGHT GOLD PRINT** for star blocks

1-1/4 yards **GOLD/BLACK PRINT** for star background

1/4 yard **MEDIUM GOLD PRINT** for Log Cabin center squares

1/4 yard *each* of **12 COORDINATING PRINTS** for Log Cabin strips

2/3 yard **BLACK PRINT** for inner border and corner squares

1-7/8 yards **GREEN PLAID** for outer border (cut on the lengthwise grain)

assortment of fat-quarters for the appliqués

2/3 yard **GOLD/BLACK PRINT** for binding

4 yards backing fabric

paper-backed fusible web for appliqués

pearl cotton or embroidery floss for decorative stitches: black and gold

1/4-inch black buttons for gingerbread men appliqués (10)

1/2-inch black buttons for snowmen appliqués (6)

quilt batting, at least 70 x 78-inches

Before beginning this project, read through **Getting Started** on page 210.

Star Blocks

Makes 20 blocks

Cutting

From **LIGHT GOLD PRINT**:

- Cut 3, 4-1/2 x 42-inch strips. From the strips cut:
  20, 4-1/2-inch squares
- Cut 10, 2-1/2 x 42-inch strips. From the strips cut:
  160, 2-1/2-inch squares

From **GOLD/BLACK PRINT**:

- Cut 14, 2-1/2 x 42-inch strips. From the strips cut:
  80, 2-1/2 x 4-1/2-inch rectangles
  80, 2-1/2-inch squares

Piecing

Step 1   With right sides together, position a 2-1/2-inch **LIGHT GOLD** square on the corner of a 2-1/2 x 4-1/2-inch **GOLD/BLACK** rectangle. Draw a diagonal line on the **LIGHT GOLD** square and stitch on the line. Trim the seam allowance to 1/4-inch; press. Repeat this process at the opposite corner of the rectangle.

Make 80

Step 2   Sew Step 1 star point units to the top/bottom edges of a 4-1/2-inch **LIGHT GOLD** square; press. Make 20 units. Sew 2-1/2-inch **GOLD/BLACK** squares to both ends of the remaining star point units; press. Sew the units to the side edges of the square units; press. At this point each star block should measure 8-1/2-inches square.

Make 20

Log Cabin Blocks

Makes 22 blocks

Cutting

From **MEDIUM GOLD PRINT**:
- Cut 2, 2-1/2 x 42-inch strips. From the strips cut: 22, 2-1/2-inch center squares

From *each* of the **12 COORDINATING PRINTS**:
- Cut 4, 1-1/2 x 42-inch strips

Piecing

Note: *You may vary the position of each* **COORDINATING PRINT** *strip as we did to get a scrappy look, or place each print in the same position in each block. Follow Steps 1 through 3 to piece each of the 22 Log Cabin blocks.*

Step 1 Sew a 1-1/2 x 42-inch **COORDINATING PRINT** strip to a 2-1/2-inch **MEDIUM GOLD** square. Press the seam allowance toward the strip just added. Trim the strip even with the edge of the **MEDIUM GOLD** center square, creating a 2-piece unit.

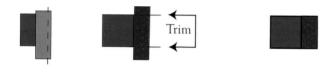

Step 2 Turn the 2-piece unit to the right a quarter turn. Stitch a different 1-1/2-inch wide **COORDINATING PRINT** strip to the 2-piece unit; press and trim.

Step 3 Continue adding 1-1/2-inch wide **COORDINATING PRINT** strips to the unit to complete the Log Cabin block. Press each seam allowance toward the strip just added, and trim each strip before adding the next. Each Log Cabin block should measure 8-1/2-inches square when completed. Adjust the seam allowances if needed.

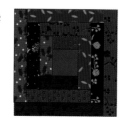

Make 22

Appliqué-Fusible Web Method

Step 1 Make templates of the appliqué shapes on pages 109–116. Trace the appliqué shapes onto the paper side of the fusible web, leaving a small margin between each shape. Cut the shapes apart.

Note: *When you are fusing a large shape, like the tree, fuse just the outer edges of the shape so that it will not look stiff when finished. To do this, draw a line about 3/8-inch inside the tree, and cut away the fusible web on this line. See* **General Instructions** *on page 210 or a generic diagram of this technique. Shapes will vary depending on the quilt design.*

Step 2 Following the manufacturer's instructions, fuse the shapes to the wrong side of the fabrics chosen for the appliqués. Let the fabric cool and cut along the traced line. Peel away the paper backing from the fusible web.

Step 3 Referring to the quilt photograph, position the shapes on the Log Cabin blocks layering them as needed. Sew 2 Log Cabin blocks together for the tree appliqué. Fuse the shapes in place.

Note: *We suggest pinning a rectangle of tear-away stabilizer to the backside of the blocks so they it will lay flat when the appliqué is complete. We use the extra-lightweight Easy Tear™ sheets as a stabilizer. When the appliqué is complete, tear away the stabilizer.*

Step 4 We machine blanket stitched around the shapes using machine embroidery thread for the top thread and regular sewing thread in the bobbin. If you like, you could hand blanket stitch around the shapes with pearl cotton. The facial features of the snowmen are done with the straight stitch and the cuffs of the mittens are done with the stem stitch. Sew buttons to the snowmen and gingerbread men.

Note: To prevent the hand blanket stitches from "rolling off" the edges of the appliqué shapes, take an extra backstitch in the same place as you made the blanket stitch, going around outer curves, corners, and points. For straight edges, taking a backstitch every inch is enough.

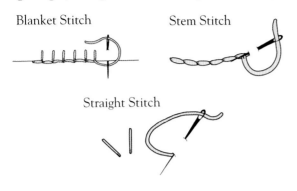

Blanket Stitch   Stem Stitch

Straight Stitch

Quilt Assembly

Step 1   Referring to the quilt diagram, sew the star blocks and the Log Cabin blocks together in 6 vertical rows. Press the seam allowances in alternating directions by rows so the seams will fit snugly together with the less bulk.

Step 2   Pin the blocks at the intersections and sew the rows together; press.

Borders

Note: *The yardage given allows for the **BLACK** inner border strips to be cut on the crosswise grain. Diagonally piece the strips as needed, referring to **Diagonal Piecing** instructions on page 215. Read through **Border** instructions on page 214 for general instructions on adding borders. The yardage given allows for the **PLAID** outer border strips to be cut on the lengthwise grain (a couple extra inches are allowed for trimming). Cutting the strips on the lengthwise grain will eliminate the need for piecing or matching the **PLAID** outer border strips.*

Cutting

From **BLACK PRINT:**
• Cut 6, 2-1/2 x 42-inch strips for the inner border
• Cut 4, 6-1/2-inch squares for corner squares

From **GREEN PLAID:**
• Cut 2, 6-1/2 x 64-inch side outer border strips
• Cut 2, 6-1/2 x 56-inch top/bottom outer border strips

Attaching the Borders

Step 1   Attach the 2-1/2-inch wide **BLACK** inner border strips.

Step 2   Attach the 6-1/2 x 56-inch **GREEN PLAID** top/bottom outer border strips. Trim the strips as needed.

Step 3   For the side outer borders, measure the quilt from top to bottom, including the seam allowances but not the borders just added. Trim the 6-1/2 x 64-inch **GREEN PLAID** outer border strips to this length. Sew the 6-1/2-inch **BLACK** corner squares to both ends of the side border strips; press. Sew the border strips to the side edges of the quilt; press.

Step 4   Referring to the quilt diagram for placement, position the appliqué shapes on the quilt top, layering them as needed; fuse in place.

Step 5   Refer to Step 4 and the decorative stitch diagrams in the **Appliqué** section to appliqué the shapes in place.

Putting It All Together

Cut the 4 yard length of backing fabric in half crosswise to make 2, 2 yard lengths. Refer to **Finishing the Quilt** on page 215 for complete instructions.

Binding

Cutting

From **GOLD/BLACK PRINT:**
• Cut 7, 2-3/4 x 42-inch strips

Sew the binding to the quilt using a 3/8-inch seam allowance. This measurement will produce a 1/2-inch wide finished double binding. Refer to **Binding and Diagonal Piecing** on page 215 for complete instructions.

Winter Memories Appliqué Templates

The appliqué shapes are reversed for
tracing purposes. When the appliqué is finished
it will appear as in the diagram.

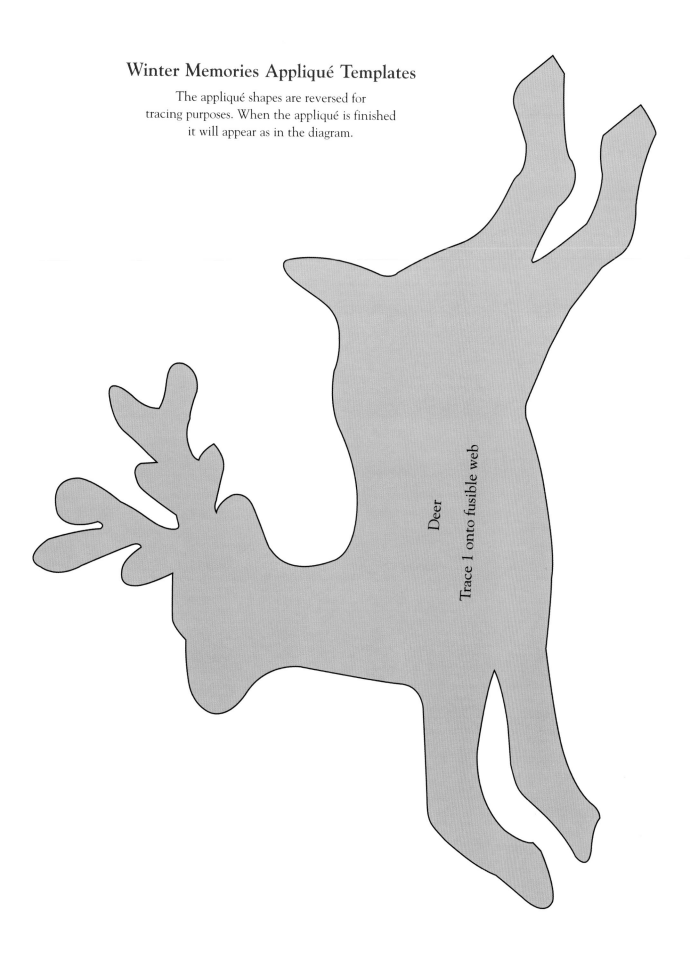

Deer

Trace 1 onto fusible web

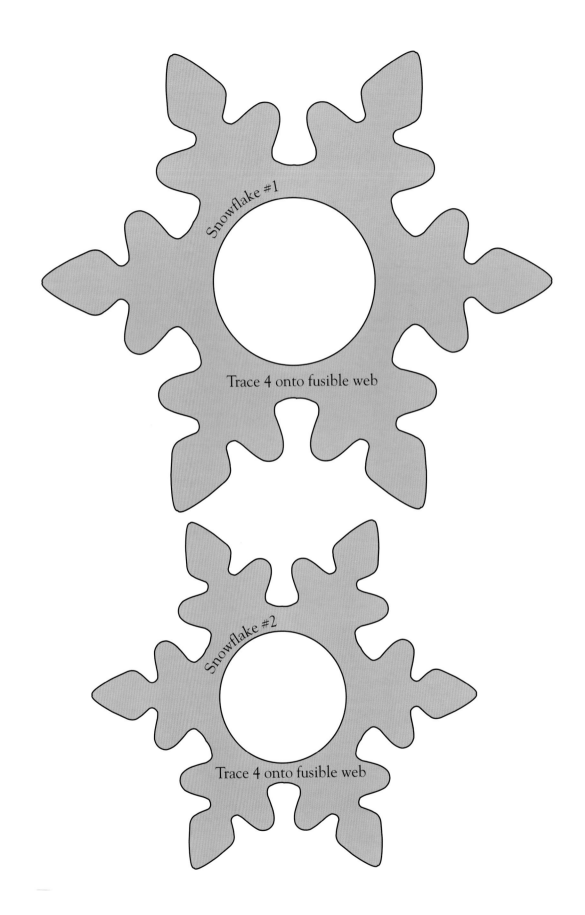

Snowflake #1

Trace 4 onto fusible web

Snowflake #2

Trace 4 onto fusible web

Tree Base

Trace 2 onto fusible web

Tree

Trace 2 onto fusible web

Bow for Wreath

Trace 2 onto fusible web

Wreath

Trace 2 onto fusible web

Mitten

Trace 2 onto fusible web

Hat

Trace 2
onto fusible web

Trace 2 onto fusible web

Gingerbread Man

Snowman

Trace 2
onto fusible web

Scarf   Trace 2 onto fusible web

114

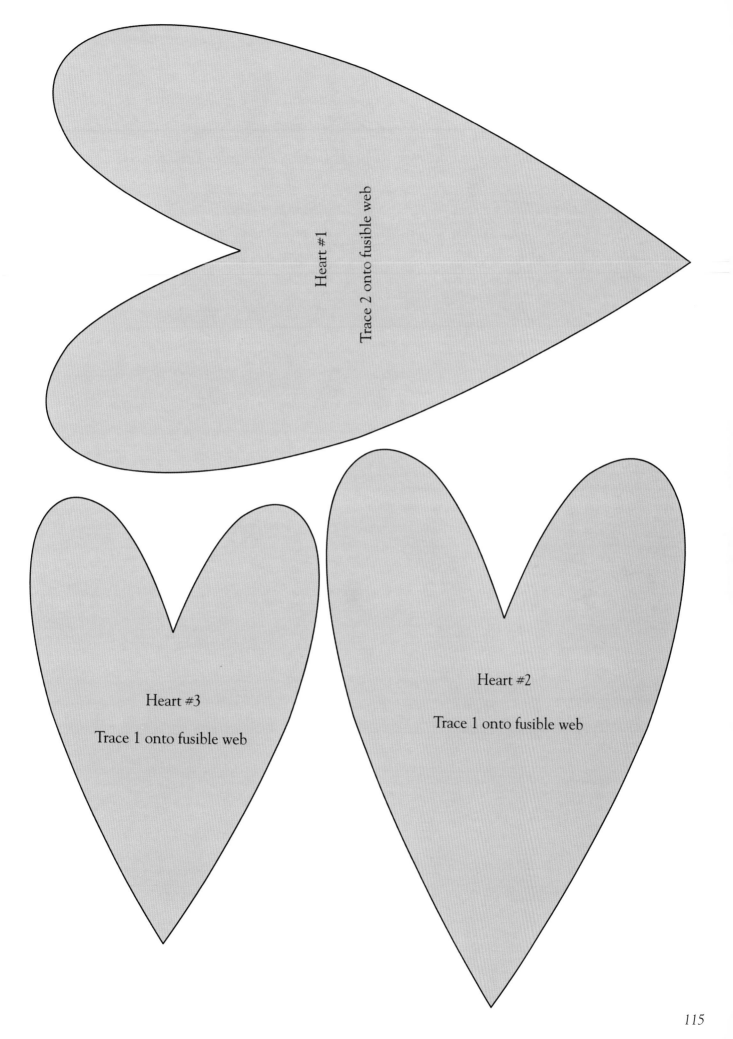

Heart #1

Trace 2 onto fusible web

Heart #3

Trace 1 onto fusible web

Heart #2

Trace 1 onto fusible web

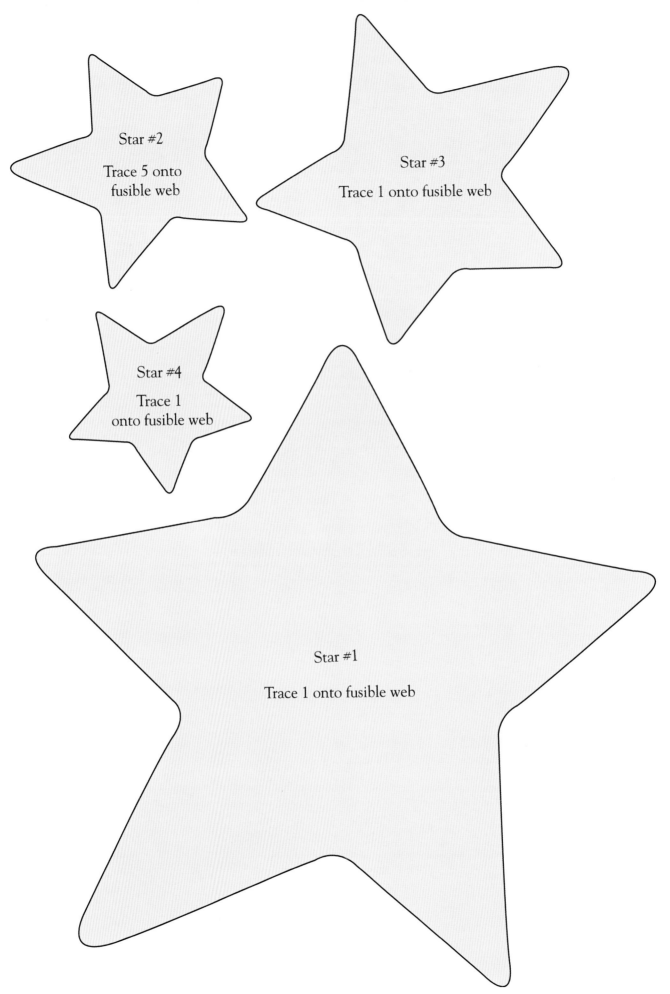

Star #2

Trace 5 onto fusible web

Star #3

Trace 1 onto fusible web

Star #4

Trace 1 onto fusible web

Star #1

Trace 1 onto fusible web

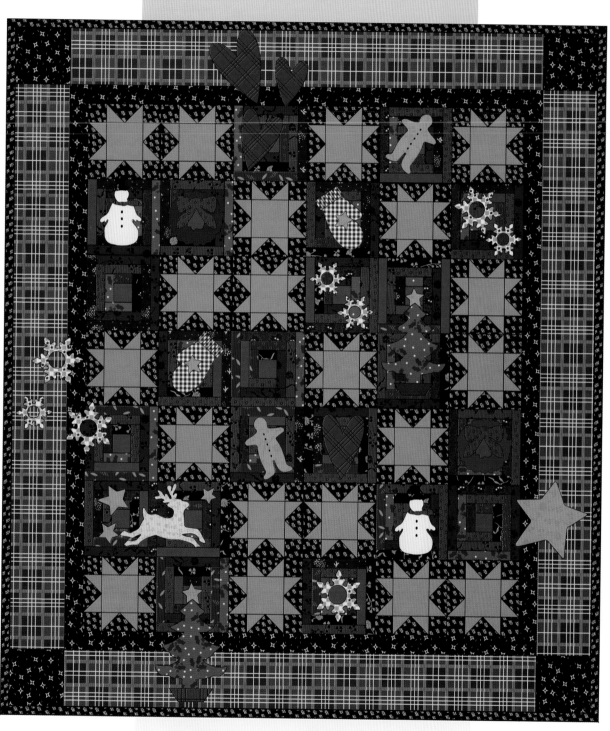

Winter Memories

64 x 72-inches

Heart Daisy Chain

To fill your room with love in bloom, start with four appliquéd sweetheart daisy chains surrounded by a pieced ribbon border. Finish with a large floral border print that gathers all the elements together.

Heart Daisy Chain

70-inches square

Fabrics & Supplies

1-1/4 yards **BEIGE PRINT** for appliqué foundation

1 yard **GREEN PRINT #1**
for lattice, inner border, and pieced border

1 yard **RED PRINT**
for pieced border and flower appliqués

1 yard **GREEN PRINT #2**
for pieced border and middle border

1-5/8 yards **RED DAISY BASKET**
for outer border

1/2 yard **GREEN PLAID**
for vine and leaf appliqués

1/8 yard **GOLD PRINT**
for flower center appliqués

3/4 yard **RED PLAID**
for binding (cut on the bias)

4-1/4 yards backing fabric

freezer paper for flower and leaf appliqués

lightweight cardboard for flower center appliqués

quilt batting, at least 76-inches square

Before beginning this project,
read through **Getting Started** on page 210.

Appliqué

Cutting

From **BEIGE PRINT:**
• Cut 2, 20-1/2 x 42-inch strips. From the strips cut:
  4, 20-1/2-inch appliqué foundation squares

Vine Appliqué

Cutting

From **GREEN PLAID:**
• Cut enough 1-3/8-inch wide **bias** strips to make 4,
  50-inch long vine strips. Diagonally piece the
  strips as needed.

Prepare the Vine

Step 1   Fold a 1-3/8-inch wide **GREEN PLAID**
strip in half lengthwise with wrong sides together;
press. To keep the raw edges aligned, stitch a scant
1/4-inch away from the edges. Fold the strip in half
again so the raw edges are hidden by the first folded
edge; press.

Step 2   Referring to the quilt diagram for
placement, position the prepared vine on a
20-1/2-inch **BEIGE** appliqué foundation square
and hand baste or pin in place. With matching
thread, hand appliqué the vine in place.

Basting Method

Tip: *We suggest laying the appliqué foundation square on a*
flat surface for pinning
and basting the vine in
place. This will help the
vine stay nice and flat.
Also, basting the vine in
a zigzag fashion makes
appliquéing so much
easier; no pins to catch
your thread.

Vine Placement Diagram

Freezer Paper Appliqué Method

Prepare the Flower and Leaf Appliqués

With this method of hand appliqué, the freezer paper forms a base around which the appliqués are shaped. The circular flower center shapes will be appliquéd using the **Cardboard Appliqué Method** below.

Step 1   Make templates using the shape on page 123. Use a pencil to trace the shapes on the paper side of the freezer paper and cut out the shapes on the traced lines.

Step 2   With a hot, dry iron, press the coated side of the freezer paper shape onto the wrong side of the fabric chosen for the appliqué.

Step 3   Cut out the shape a scant 1/4-inch beyond the edge of the freezer paper pattern.

Step 4   Referring to the quilt diagram, position and pin the prepared flower and leaf shapes on the appliqué foundation squares. With your needle, turn the seam allowance over the edge of the freezer paper shape and hand stitch in place. When there is about 3/4-inch left to appliqué, slide your needle into this opening, loosen the freezer paper from the fabric, and gently pull the freezer paper out. Finish stitching the appliqué in place.

Cardboard Appliqué Method

Prepare the Flower Center Appliqués

Step 1   Make a cardboard template using the flower center pattern on page 123.

Step 2   Position the flower center template on the wrong side of the fabric chosen for the appliqué and trace around the template 16 times, leaving a 3/4-inch margin around each shape. Remove the template and cut a scant 1/4-inch beyond the drawn lines.

Step 3   To create smooth, round circles, run a line of basting stitches around each circle, placing the

stitches halfway between the drawn line and the cut edge of the circle. After basting, keep the needle and thread attached for the next step.

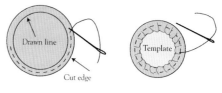

Make 16 flower centers

Step 4   Place the cardboard template on the wrong side of the fabric circle and tug on the basting stitches, gathering the fabric over the template. When the thread is tight, space the gathers evenly and make a knot to secure the thread. Clip the thread, press the circle, and remove the cardboard template. Continue this process to make 16 flower centers.

Step 5   Hand appliqué the flower centers to the flowers with matching thread.

Quilt Center

Cutting

From **GREEN PRINT #1:**
- Cut 1, 2-1/2 x 42-inch strip. From the strip cut:
     2, 2-1/2 x 20-1/2-inch lattice strips
- Cut 1, 2-1/2 x **42-1/2-inch** lattice strip

Quilt Center Assembly

Referring to the quilt diagram, sew an appliquéd block to both side edges of the 2-1/2 x 20-1/2-inch **GREEN PRINT #1** lattice strips; press. Make 2 block rows. Sew the block rows to both side edges of the 2-1/2 x **42-1/2-inch GREEN PRINT #1** lattice strip; press. At this point the quilt center should measure 42-1/2-inches square.

Borders

Note: *The yardage given allows for the border strips to be cut on the crosswise grain. Diagonally piece the strips as needed, referring to* **Diagonal Piecing** *instructions on page 215. Read through* **Border** *instructions on page 214 for general instructions on adding borders.*

Cutting

From GREEN PRINT #1:
- Cut 5, 3-1/2 x 42-inch inner border strips
- Cut 3, 2-1/2 x 42-inch strips.
  From the strips cut:
  48, 2-1/2-inch squares

From RED PRINT:
- Cut 6, 2-1/2 x 42-inch strips.
  From the strips cut:
  48, 2-1/2 x 4-1/2-inch rectangles
  4, 2-1/2-inch corner squares

From GREEN PRINT #2:
- Cut 6, 3-1/2 x 42-inch middle border strips
- Cut 3, 2-1/2 x 42-inch strips.
  From the strips cut:
  48, 2-1/2-inch squares

From RED DAISY BASKET:
- Cut 8, 6-1/2 x 42-inch outer border strips

Assembling and Attaching the Borders

Step 1   Attach the 3-1/2-inch wide **GREEN PRINT #1** inner border strips.

Step 2   With right sides together, position a 2-1/2-inch **GREEN PRINT #1** square on the right corner of a 2-1/2 x 4-1/2-inch **RED** rectangle. Draw a diagonal line on the square and stitch on the line. Trim the seam allowance to 1/4-inch; press. Repeat this process at the opposite corner of the rectangle using a 2-1/2-inch **GREEN PRINT #2** square.

Make 24

Step 3   With right sides together, position a 2-1/2-inch **GREEN PRINT #1** square on the left corner of a 2-1/2 x 4-1/2-inch **RED** rectangle. Draw a diagonal line on the **GREEN PRINT #1** square; stitch, trim, and press. Repeat this process at the opposite corner of the rectangle using a 2-1/2-inch **GREEN PRINT #2** square.

Make 24

Step 4   Referring to the diagram for placement, sew the Step 2 and 3 units together in pairs; press.

Make 24

Step 5   For each of the pieced borders, sew together 6 of the Step 4 units; press. <u>At this point each pieced border should measure 2-1/2 x 48-1/2-inches.</u>

Make 4

Step 6   Sew pieced border strips to the top/bottom edges of the quilt center; press. Sew the 2-1/2-inch **RED PRINT** corner squares to both ends of the remaining pieced border strips; press. Sew the border strips to the side edges of the quilt center; press.

Step 7   Attach the 3-1/2-inch wide **GREEN PRINT #2** middle border strips.

Step 8   Attach the 6-1/2-inch wide **RED DAISY BASKET** outer border strips.

Putting It All Together

Cut the 4-1/4 yard length of backing fabric in half crosswise to make 2, 2-1/8 yard lengths. Refer to **Finishing the Quilt** on page 215 for complete instructions.

Binding

Cutting

From RED PLAID:
- Cut enough 2-3/4-inch wide **bias** strips to make a 300-inch long strip.

Sew the binding to the quilt using a 3/8-inch seam allowance. This measurement will produce a 1/2-inch wide finished double binding. Refer to **Binding and Diagonal Piecing** on page 215 for complete instructions.

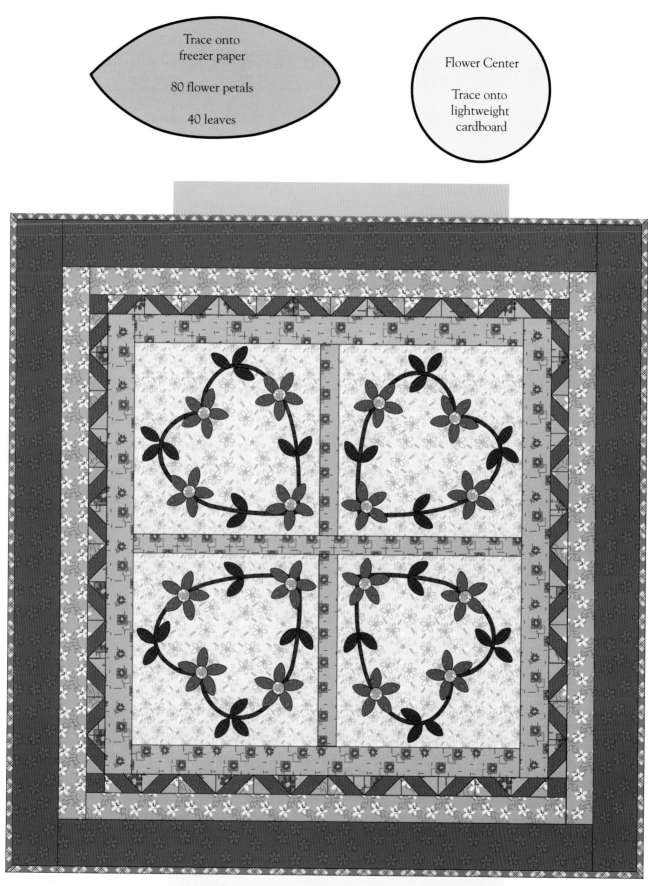

Trace onto
freezer paper

80 flower petals

40 leaves

Flower Center

Trace onto
lightweight
cardboard

Heart Daisy Chain

70-inches square

Bedtime

BLISS

ransform any room into a restful retreat and take a sabbatical from stress—on a daily basis!

Whether it's breakfast in bed, an afternoon nap, or a blissful evening with a good book, snuggling up in an inviting quilt makes it even more memorable. To fill your rooms with soft comfort, choose from any of the eye-catching quilts featured on the following pages.

Sunwashed Log Cabin

Beige

An old window frame (minus the glass) is softened by a dried-flower wreath for wall decor that blends beautifully with a vintage bed. In keeping with the feeling of comfort and quiet, whisper-soft shades of beige prints create an unusual Log Cabin quilt.

Sunwashed Log Cabin

Beige

84 x 98-inches

Fabrics & Supplies

3/8 yard **CORAL PRINT** for center squares

7/8 yard **TAN PRINT #1** for Log Cabin strips

1-1/2 yards **TAN PRINT #2** for Log Cabin strips

2-1/4 yards **TAN PRINT #3** for Log Cabin strips

1-1/8 yards **BEIGE PRINT #1**
for Log Cabin strips

1-7/8 yards **BEIGE PRINT #2**
for Log Cabin strips

2-2/3 yards **BEIGE PRINT #3**
for Log Cabin strips

1 yard **ROSE PLAID**
for binding (cut on the bias)

7-1/2 yards backing fabric

quilt batting, at least 90 x 104-inches

Before beginning this project,
read through **Getting Started** on page 210.

Log Cabin Blocks

Makes 168 blocks

Cutting

From **CORAL PRINT:**
- Cut 6, 1-1/2 x 42-inch strips

From **TAN PRINT #1:**
- Cut 6, 1-1/2 x 42-inch strips
- Cut 11 more 1-1/2 x 42-inch strips

From **TAN PRINT #2:**
- Cut 33, 1-1/2 x 42-inch strips

From **TAN PRINT #3:**
- Cut 52, 1-1/2 x 42-inch strips

From **BEIGE PRINT #1:**
- Cut 25, 1-1/2 x 42-inch strips

From **BEIGE PRINT #2:**
- Cut 43, 1-1/2 x 42-inch strips

From **BEIGE PRINT #3:**
- Cut 62, 1-1/2 x 42-inch strips

Piecing

Note: *You may vary the position of the* **TAN PRINT** *fabrics from block to block, or place them in the same position in each block. The same is true of the* **BEIGE PRINT** *fabrics. Follow Steps 1 through 5 to piece each of the 168 Log Cabin blocks.*

Step 1   Aligning long edges, sew the 1-1/2-inch wide **CORAL** and **TAN #1** strip together in pairs; press. Make a total of 6 strip sets. Cut the strip sets into segments.

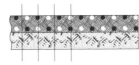

Crosscut 168, 1-1/2-inch wide segments

Step 2   Sew a 1-1/2-inch wide **TAN #1** strip to the 2-piece unit. Press the seam allowance toward the strip just added. Trim the strip even with the edges of the 2-piece unit.

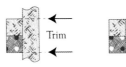

Trim

Step 3 Turn the unit a quarter turn to the left. Sew a 1-1/2-inch wide **BEIGE #1** strip to the unit; press and trim.

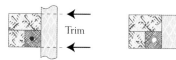

Step 4 Turn the unit a quarter turn to the left. Sew a 1-1/2-inch wide **BEIGE #1** strip to the unit; press and trim.

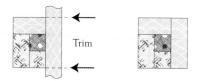

Step 5 Referring to the block diagram for placement, continue this process by adding 1-1/2-inch wide strips of **TAN #2, BEIGE #2, TAN #3,** and **BEIGE #3** to complete the Log Cabin block. Press each seam allowance toward the strip just added; trim each strip before adding the next. Each Log Cabin block should measure 7-1/2-inches square when completed. Adjust the seam allowances if needed.

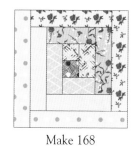

Make 168

Quilt Center

Step 1 Referring to the quilt diagram for block placement, sew the Log Cabin blocks together in 14 rows of 12 blocks each. Press the seam allowances in alternating directions by rows so the seams will fit snugly together with less bulk.

Step 2 Pin the rows at the block intersections; sew the rows together and press.

Putting It All Together

Cut the 7-1/2 yard length of backing fabric in thirds crosswise to make 3, 2-1/2 yard lengths. Refer to **Finishing the Quilt** on page 215 for complete instructions.

Binding

Cutting

From **ROSE PLAID:**
• Cut enough 2-1/2-inch wide **bias** strips to make a 380-inch long strip.

Sew the binding to the quilt using a scant 1/4-inch seam allowance. This measurement will produce a 1/4-inch wide finished double binding. Refer to **Binding and Diagonal Piecing** on page 215 for complete instructions.

Sunwashed Log Cabin
Beige
84 x 98-inches

Sunwashed Log Cabin

Pastel

98 x 112-inches

Fabrics & Supplies

3/8 yard **GOLD PRINT** for center squares

1-2/3 yard *each* of **6 ASSORTED PASTEL PRINTS** for Log Cabin strips

1-2/3 yard *each* of **6 ASSORTED BEIGE PRINTS** for Log Cabin strips

1 yard **GOLD PRINT** for binding

8-2/3 yards backing fabric

quilt batting, at least 104 x 118-inches

Before beginning this project, read through **Getting Started** on page 210.

Log Cabin Blocks

Makes 224 blocks

Cutting

From **GOLD PRINT:**
• Cut 9, 1-1/2 x 42-inch strips

From **6 ASSORTED PASTEL PRINTS:**
• Cut 38, 1-1/2 x 42-inch strips from *each* fabric

From **6 ASSORTED BEIGE PRINTS:**
• Cut 38, 1-1/2 x 42-inch strips from *each* fabric

Piecing

Note: *You may vary the position of the **PASTEL PRINT** fabrics from block to block, or place them in the same position in each block. The same is true of the **BEIGE PRINT** fabrics. Follow Steps 1 through 5 to piece each of the 224 Log Cabin blocks.*

Step 1 Aligning long edges, sew a 1-1/2-inch wide **GOLD** and **PASTEL** strip together; press. Repeat with the **GOLD** and **ASSORTED PASTEL** strips to make a total of 9 strip sets. Cut the strip sets into segments.

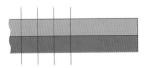

Crosscut 224, 1-1/2-inch wide segments

Step 2 Sew a 1-1/2-inch wide **PASTEL** strip to the 2-piece unit. Press the seam allowance toward the strip just added. Trim the strip even with the edges of the 2-piece unit.

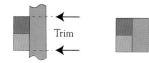

Step 3 Turn the unit a quarter turn to the left. Sew a 1-1/2-inch wide **BEIGE** strip to the unit; press and trim.

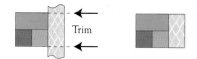

Step 4 Turn the unit a quarter turn to the left. Sew a 1-1/2-inch wide **BEIGE** strip to the unit; press.

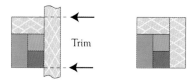

Step 5 Referring to the block diagram for placement, continue this process by adding 1-1/2-inch wide strips of **ASSORTED BEIGE** and **PASTEL PRINTS** to complete the Log Cabin block. Press each seam allowance toward the strip just added and trim each strip before adding the next. Each Log Cabin block should measure 7-1/2-inches square when completed. Adjust the seam allowances if needed.

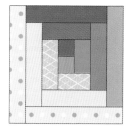

Make 224

Quilt Center

Step 1 Referring to the quilt diagram for block placement, sew the Log Cabin blocks together in 16 rows of 14 blocks each. Press the seam allowances in alternating directions by rows so the seams will fit snugly together with less bulk.

Step 2 Pin the rows at the block intersections; sew the rows together. Press the seam allowances in one direction.

Putting It All Together

Cut the 8-2/3 yard length of backing fabric in thirds crosswise to make 3, 2-7/8 yard lengths. Refer to **Finishing the Quilt** on page 215 for complete instructions.

Binding

Cutting

From **GOLD PRINT:**
• Cut 11, 2-1/2 x 42-inch strips

Sew the binding to the quilt using a scant 1/4-inch seam allowance. This measurement will produce a 1/4-inch wide finished double binding. Refer to **Binding and Diagonal Piecing** on page 215 for complete instructions.

Sunwashed Log Cabin
Pastel
98 x 112-inches

Harvest Bounty

An iron plant cage serves as a basket for pumpkins and gourds—a unique way to display pumpkins that are inspiration for the life-sized appliquéd replicas surrounding the pieced blocks of Harvest Bounty. In the quilt, layers of rich colors in quiet prints create an impressive tribute to autumn.

Harvest Bounty

74 x 96-inches

Fabrics & Supplies

7/8 yard **BROWN BERRY PRINT**
for 4-patch centers and inner border

3/8 yard **LIGHT GREEN SMALL LEAF PRINT**
for 4-patch centers

5/8 yard **GREEN PRINT #1**
for sawtooth sections

7/8 yard **CREAM PRINT**
for pieced block background

3/8 yard *each* of 4 **COORDINATING
MEDIUM/DARK PRINTS** for block borders

1-1/2 yards **BEIGE LEAF PRINT**
for side and corner triangles

5/8 yard **TAN SMALL LEAF PRINT**
for first middle border

5/8 yard **GREEN PRINT #2**
for second middle border

2-1/2 yards **RED FLORAL** for outer border

7/8 yard **DARK RED PRINT** for binding

5-3/4 yards backing fabric

quilt batting, at least 80 x 102-inches

Before beginning this project,
read through **Getting Started** on page 210.

Optional Appliqué

1/2 yard **ORANGE PRINT #1**
for pumpkin appliqués (outer sections)

1/3 yard **ORANGE PRINT #2**
for pumpkin appliqués (top and side sections)

1/3 yard **ORANGE PRINT #3**
for pumpkin appliqués (center sections)

1/2 yard **DARK GREEN LEAF PRINT**
for leaf and vine appliqués

1/3 yard **GREEN PRINT #1**
for leaf and stem appliqués

freezer paper for appliqués

template material for appliqués

pearl cotton for decorative stitches: black

Pieced Blocks

Makes 8 blocks

Cutting

From **BROWN BERRY PRINT**:
• Cut 2, 4-1/2 x 42-inch strips

From **LIGHT GREEN SMALL LEAF PRINT**:
• Cut 2, 4-1/2 x 42-inch strips

From **GREEN PRINT #1**:
• Cut 3, 2-7/8 x 42-inch strips
• Cut 4, 2-1/2 x 42-inch strips. From the strips cut:
   64, 2-1/2-inch squares

From **CREAM PRINT**:
• Cut 3, 2-7/8 x 42-inch strips
• Cut 6, 2-1/2 x 42-inch strips. From the strips cut:
   32, 2-1/2 x 4-1/2-inch rectangles
   32, 2-1/2-inch squares

From *each* of the 4 **COORDINATING
MEDIUM/DARK PRINTS**
(number the fabrics 1 through 4):
• Cut 4, 2-1/2 x 42-inch strips

Piecing

Step 1 Aligning long edges, sew the 4-1/2-inch wide **BROWN BERRY** and **LIGHT GREEN SMALL LEAF** strips together in pairs. Press, referring to **Hints and Helps for Pressing Strip Sets** on page 214. Make a total of 2 strip sets. Cut the strip sets into segments.

Crosscut 16, 4-1/2-inch wide segments

Step 2 Sew the Step 1 segments together in pairs; press. <u>At this point each 4-patch center should measure 8-1/2-inches square.</u>

Make 8

Step 3 With right sides together, layer the 2-7/8 x 42-inch **GREEN #1** and **CREAM** strips in pairs. Press together, but do not sew. Cut the layered strips into squares. Cut the layered squares in half diagonally to make 64 sets of triangles. Stitch 1/4-inch from the diagonal edge of each pair of triangles; press.

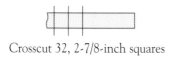

Crosscut 32, 2-7/8-inch squares

Make 64, 2-1/2-inch triangle-pieced squares

Step 4 With right sides together, position a 2-1/2-inch **GREEN #1** square on the corner of a 2-1/2 x 4-1/2-inch **CREAM** rectangle. Draw a diagonal line on the square and stitch on the line. Trim the seam allowance to 1/4-inch; press. Repeat this process at the opposite corner of the rectangle.

Make 32

Step 5 Sew Step 3 triangle-pieced squares to both side edges of the Step 4 units; press. <u>At this point each unit should measure 2-1/2 x 8-1/2-inches.</u>

Make 32

Step 6 Sew Step 5 units to the top/bottom edges of the 4-patch centers; press. Sew 2-1/2-inch **CREAM** squares to the remaining Step 5 units; press. Sew the units to the side edges of the 4-patch centers; press. <u>At this point each block should measure 12-1/2-inches square.</u>

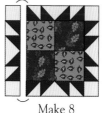

Make 8

Step 7 Sew the 2-1/2-inch wide **4 COORDINATING MEDIUM/DARK PRINT** block border strips to the edges of the Step 6 blocks in a Log Cabin fashion. Referring to the diagram below, sew a **#1** strip to the block. Press the seam allowances toward the strip just added and trim the strip even with the block.

Step 8 Turn the unit a quarter turn to the left and sew a **#2** strip to the block; press and trim.

Step 9 Turn the unit a quarter turn to the left and sew a **#3** strip to the block; press and trim. Add the **#4** strip in the same fashion. <u>At this point each block should measure 16-1/2-inches square.</u>

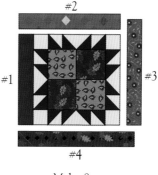

Make 8

Quilt Center

Note: The side and corner triangles are larger than necessary and will be trimmed before the borders are added.

Cutting

From **BEIGE LEAF PRINT**:
- Cut 2, 25 x 42-inch strips. From the strips cut:
  2, 25-inch squares. Cut the squares diagonally into quarters to make 8 triangles. Only 6 will be used for side triangles.
  2, 14-inch squares. Cut the squares in half diagonally to make 4 corner triangles.

Quilt Center Assembly

Step 1 Referring to the quilt diagram for block placement, sew the pieced blocks and **BEIGE LEAF** side triangles together in 4 diagonal rows. Press the seam allowances in alternating directions by rows so the seams will fit snugly together with less bulk.

Step 2 Pin the rows at the block intersections; sew the rows together. Press the seam allowances in one direction.

Step 3 Sew the corner triangles to the quilt center; press.

Step 4 Trim away the excess fabric from the side and corner triangles taking care to allow a 1/4-inch seam allowance beyond the corners of each block. Refer to **Trimming Side and Corner Triangles** on page 212 for complete instructions.

Borders

*Note: The yardage given allows for the border strips to be cut on the crosswise grain. Diagonally piece the strips as needed, referring to **Diagonal Piecing** instructions on page 215 for complete instructions. Read through **Border** instructions on page 214 for general instructions on adding borders.*

Cutting

From **BROWN BERRY PRINT**:
- Cut 7, 2-1/2 x 42-inch inner border strips

From **TAN SMALL LEAF PRINT**:
- Cut 7, 2-1/2 x 42-inch first middle border strips

From **GREEN PRINT #2**:
- Cut 7, 2-1/2 x 42-inch second middle border strips

From **RED FLORAL**:
- Cut 10, 8-1/2 x 42-inch outer border strips

Attaching the Borders

Step 1 Attach the 2-1/2-inch wide **BROWN BERRY** inner border strips.

Step 2 Attach the 2-1/2-inch wide **TAN SMALL LEAF** first middle border strips.

Step 3 Attach the 2-1/2-inch wide **GREEN #2** second middle border strips.

Step 4 Attach the 8-1/2-inch wide **RED FLORAL** outer border strips.

Appliqué

Vine Appliqué

Cutting

From **DARK GREEN LEAF PRINT**:
- Cut 6, 1-3/8 x 18-inch **bias** strips. Diagonally piece the strips as needed.

Prepare the Vines

Fold each 1-3/8-inch wide **DARK GREEN LEAF** strip in half lengthwise with wrong sides together; press. To keep the raw edges aligned, stitch a scant 1/4-inch away from the raw edges. Fold each strip in half again so the raw edges are hidden by the first folded edge; press. Set the prepared vines aside.

Freezer Paper Appliqué Method

Prepare the Pumpkin, Stem, and Leaf Appliqués

With this method of hand appliqué, the freezer paper forms a base around which the appliqués are shaped.

Step 1   Make templates using the shapes on pages 138–141. Trace the shapes on the paper side of the freezer paper the number of times indicated on each pattern. Cut out the shapes on the traced lines.

Step 2   With a hot, dry iron, press the coated side of each freezer paper shape onto the wrong side of the fabric chosen for the appliqués. Allow at least 1/2-inch between each shape for seam allowances.

Step 3   Cut out each shape a scant 1/4-inch beyond the edge of the freezer paper pattern.

Step 4   Referring to the quilt diagram, position 4 of the prepared vines and the A and B leaves on the corners of the quilt top overlapping them as shown. Pin and baste in place, referring to the basting diagram on page 39. Basting the vines in this zigzag fashion will hold them nice and flat. Hand stitch the vines in place with matching thread. With your needle, turn the seam allowance over the edge of the freezer paper leaf shape; hand stitch the leaves in place. When there is about 3/4-inch left to appliqué, slide your needle into this opening, loosen the freezer paper from the fabric, and gently pull the freezer paper out. Finish stitching the appliqués in place.

Tip: We suggest layering the quilt top on a flat surface for pinning and basting the vine in place. Basting the vine makes appliquéing so much easier; no pins to catch your thread.

Step 5   Referring to the quilt diagram on page 143, position the remaining vines and the A and B leaves on the sides of the quilt top overlapping them as shown. Pin and baste in place, referring to the basting diagram. Hand appliqué the vines in place with matching thread.

Step 6   Referring to the quilt diagram, position the pumpkin and stem shapes on the quilt top overlapping them as shown; pin in place. Hand appliqué the shapes in place with matching thread.

Putting It All Together

Cut the 5-3/4 yard length of backing fabric in half crosswise to make 2, 2-7/8 yard lengths. Refer to **Finishing the Quilt** on page 215 for complete instructions.

Binding

Cutting

From **DARK RED PRINT:**
• Cut 9, 2-3/4 x 42-inch strips

Sew the binding to the quilt using a 3/8-inch seam allowance. This measurement will produce a 1/2-inch wide finished double binding. Refer to **Binding and Diagonal Piecing** instructions on page 215.

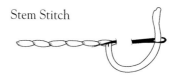

Stem Stitch

Harvest Bounty
Appliqué Templates

The appliqué shapes are reversed
for tracing purposes.
When the appliqué is finished it
will appear as in the diagram.

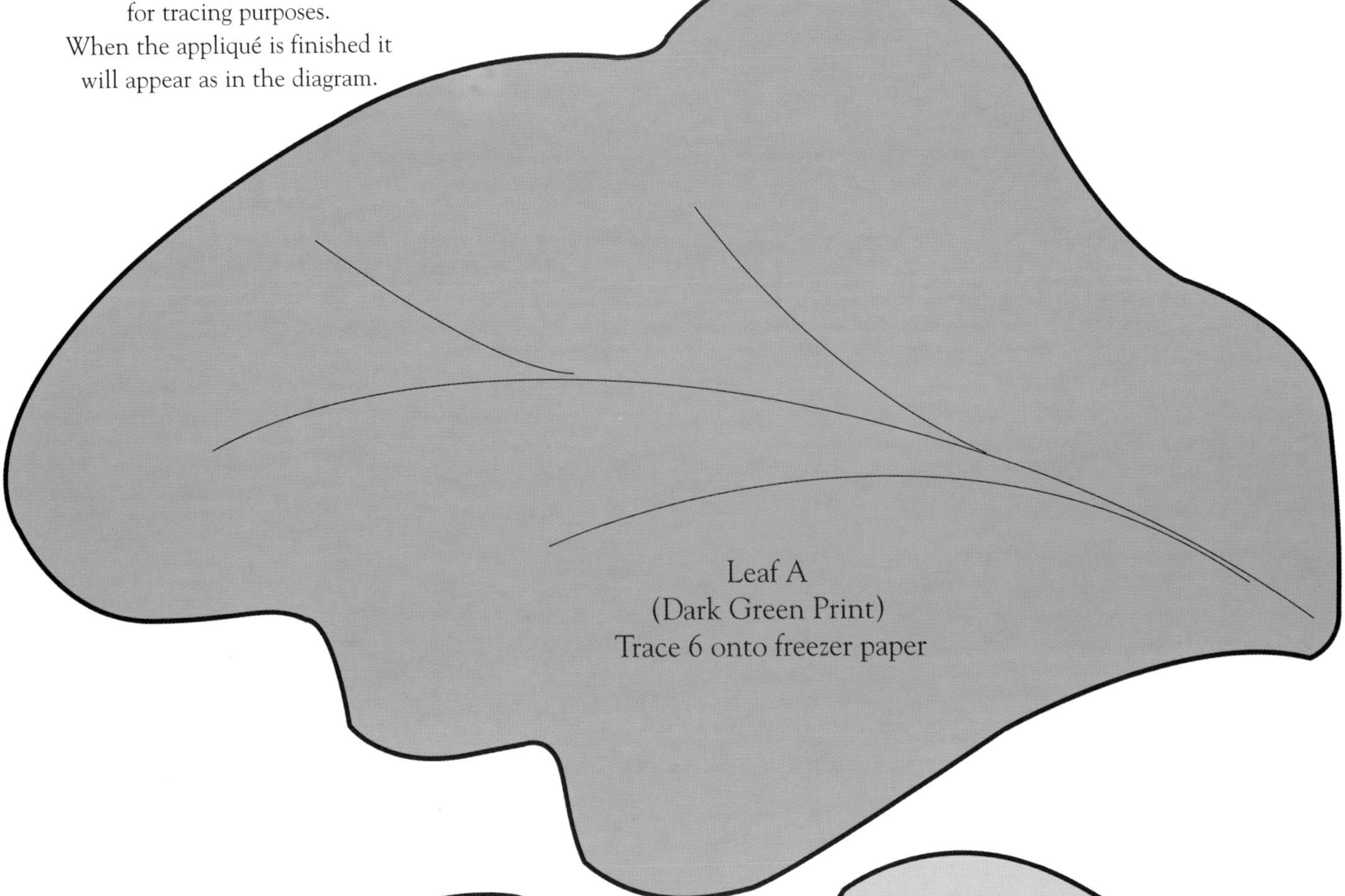

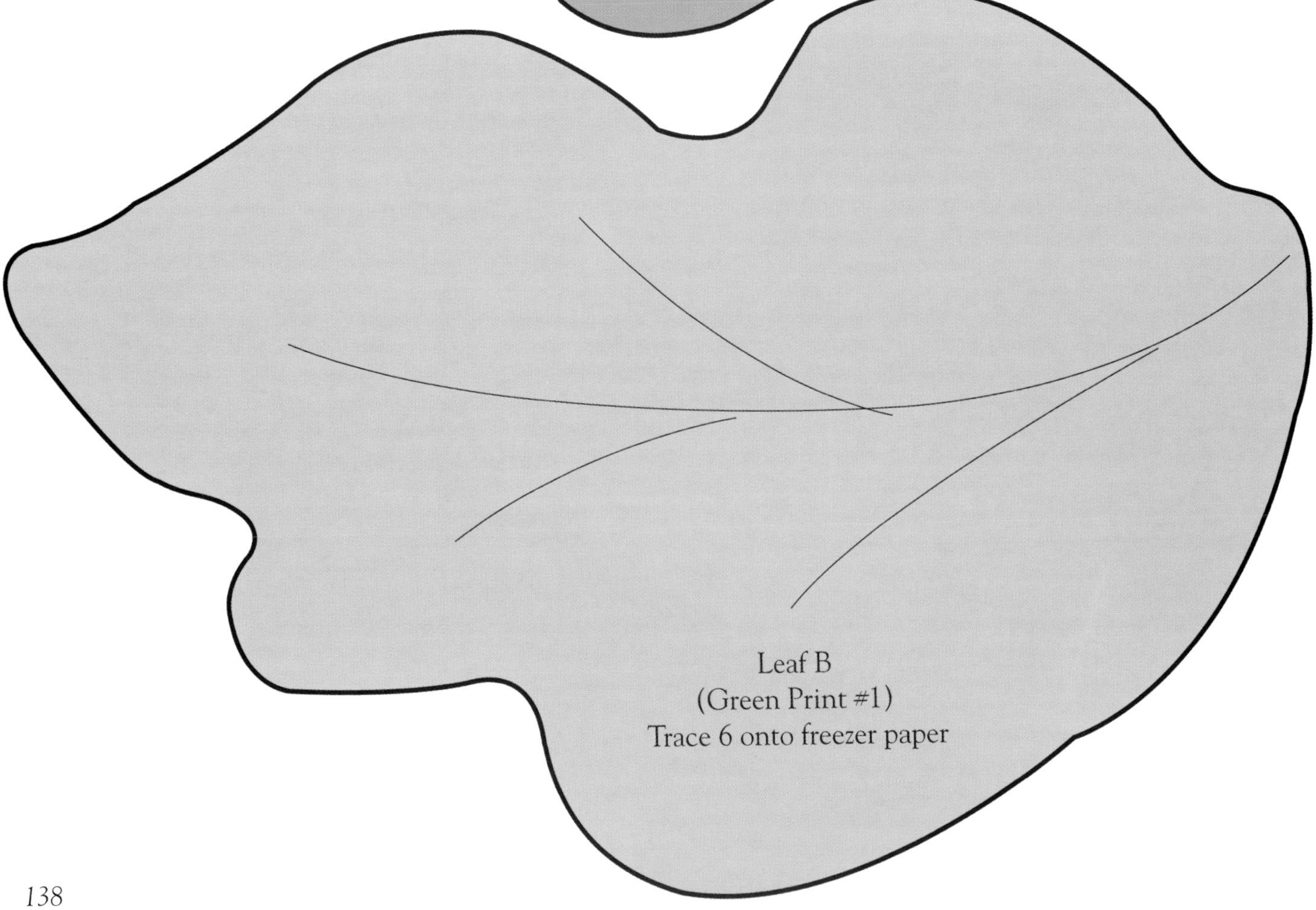

Leaf A
(Dark Green Print)
Trace 6 onto freezer paper

Leaf B
(Green Print #1)
Trace 6 onto freezer paper

Harvest Bounty Appliqué Templates

The appliqué shapes are reversed for tracing purposes. When the appliqué is finished it will appear as in the diagram.

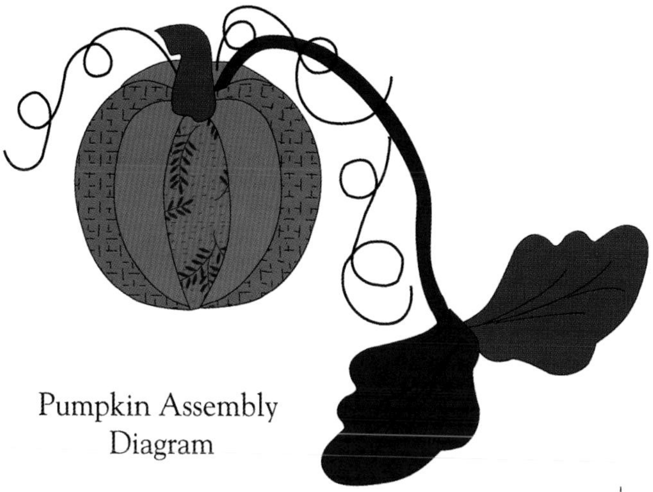

Pumpkin Assembly Diagram

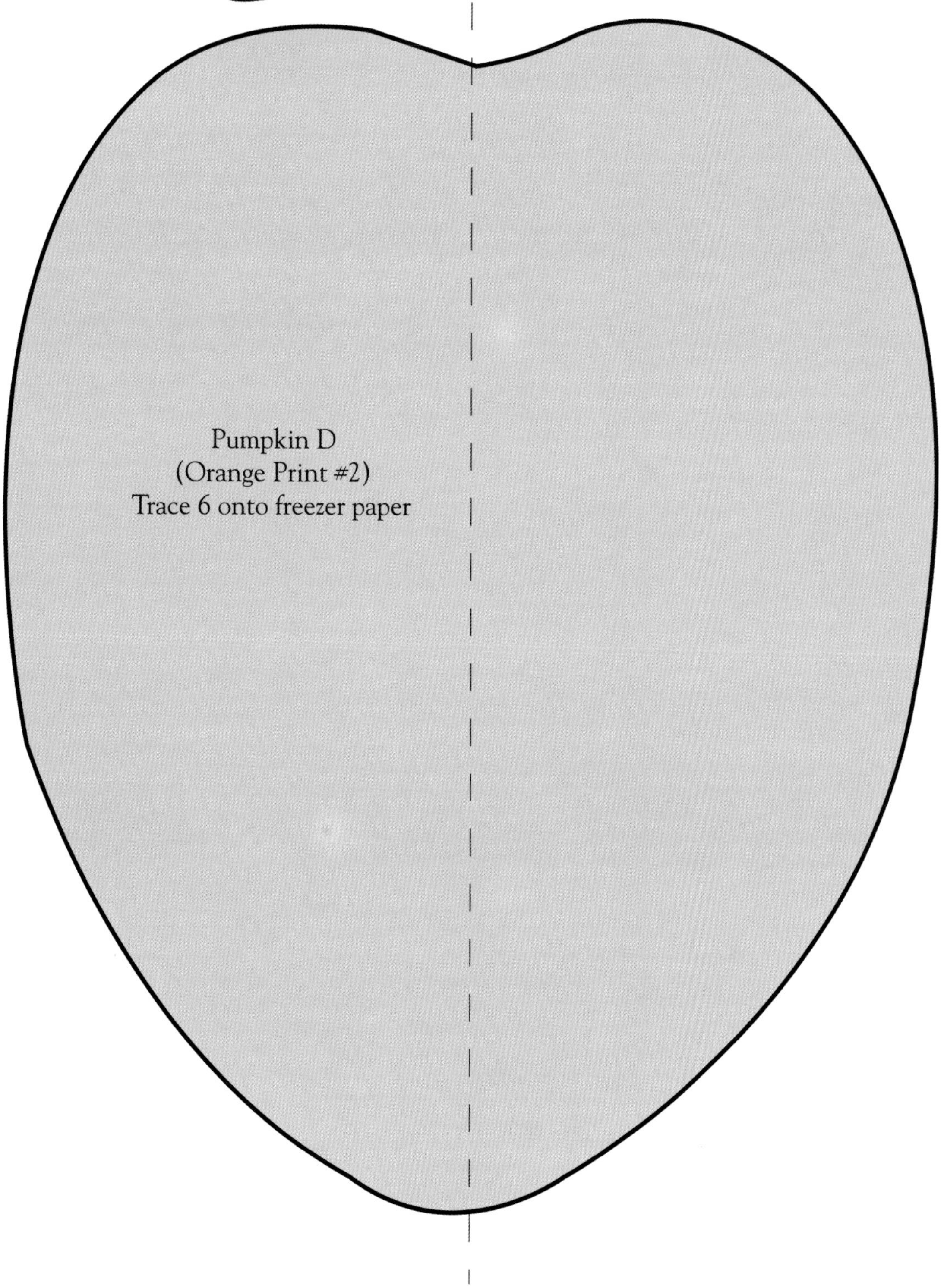
Pumpkin D
(Orange Print #2)
Trace 6 onto freezer paper

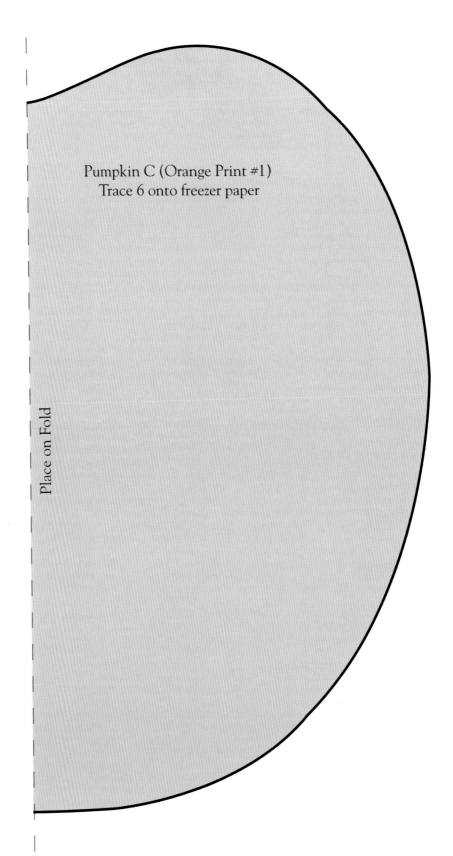

Pumpkin C (Orange Print #1)
Trace 6 onto freezer paper

Place on Fold

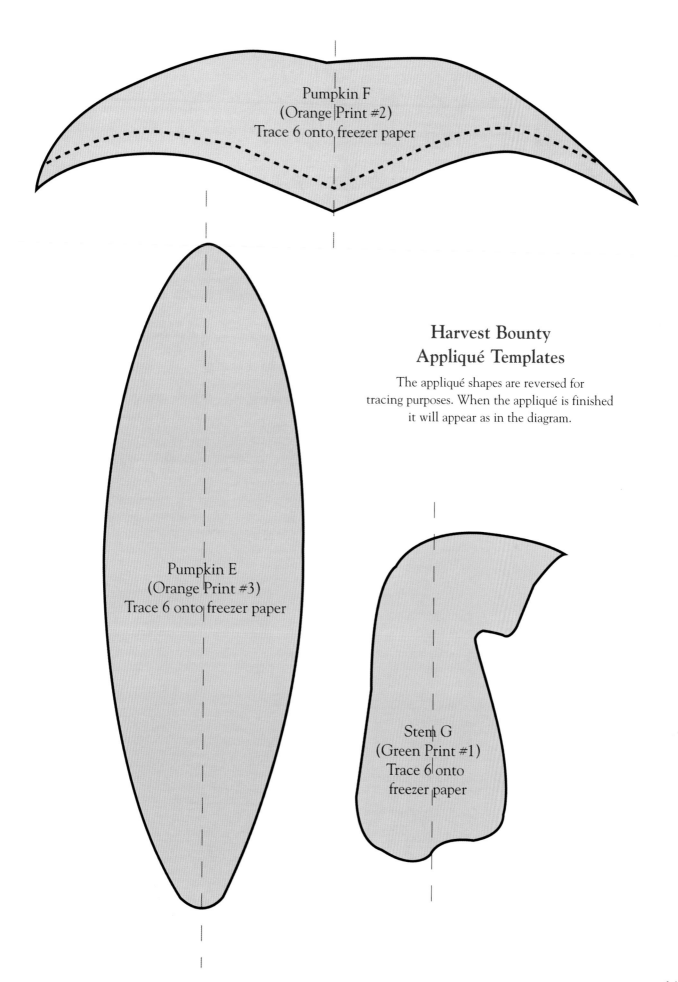

Pumpkin F
(Orange Print #2)
Trace 6 onto freezer paper

**Harvest Bounty
Appliqué Templates**

The appliqué shapes are reversed for
tracing purposes. When the appliqué is finished
it will appear as in the diagram.

Pumpkin E
(Orange Print #3)
Trace 6 onto freezer paper

Stem G
(Green Print #1)
Trace 6 onto
freezer paper

Harvest Bounty

74 x 96-inches

Northern Lights

Restful shades of deep red and forest green are combined in the standard decorating practice of blending prints, plaids, and solids—making Northern Lights a perfect scrap-happy quilt. Randomly-pieced triangles separated by lattice strips create bits of color darting throughout the quilt.

Northern Lights

72 x 90-inches

Fabrics & Supplies

3/4 yard *each* of 7 COORDINATING PRINTS
for triangle-pieced squares

1-5/8 yards BLACK PRINT
for lattice and inner border

2-1/4 yards GREEN PLAID
for outer border (cut on the lengthwise grain)

1/3 yard GREEN PRINT for corner squares

1 yard RED PRINT for binding

5-5/8 yards backing fabric

quilt batting, at least 78 x 96-inches

Before beginning this project,
read through **Getting Started** on page 210.

Triangle-Pieced Square Blocks

Makes 84 blocks

Cutting

From *each* of the 7 COORDINATING PRINTS:
• Cut at least 13, 6-7/8-inch squares from each of the
fabrics. Cut the squares in half diagonally to
make triangles. You will have extra triangles to
mix and match to get the look you want.

Piecing

Step 1 With right sides together, randomly sew
together the triangles in pairs to make 84, 6-1/2-inch
triangle-pieced squares; press.

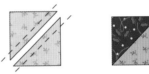

Make 84, 6-1/2-inch triangle-pieced squares

Step 2 Sew the triangle-pieced squares together in
7 rows with 12 triangle-pieced squares in each row;
press. Referring to the quilt diagram, alternate the
direction of the angles; press. <u>At this point each
block row should measure 6-1/2 x 72-1/2-inches.</u>

Quilt Center and Inner Border

Note: *The yardage given allows for the lattice/border strips to
be cut on the crosswise grain. Diagonally piece the strips as
needed, referring to* **Diagonal Piecing** *instructions on page
215. Read through* **Border** *instructions on page 214 for
general instructions on adding borders.*

Cutting

From BLACK PRINT:
• Cut 20, 2-1/2 x 42-inch lattice strips/inner
border strips

Quilt Center Assembly

Step 1 Diagonally piece the 2-1/2 x 42-inch
BLACK lattice strips together in pairs.

Step 2 Cut 8 of the 2-1/2-inch wide BLACK
lattice strips/side inner border strips to 72-1/2-inches
long (or the length of the block rows).

Step 3   Pin and sew together the 7 block rows and the 8 lattice strips/side inner border strips; press.

Step 4   Measure the quilt from left to right through the center to determine the length of the top/bottom inner borders. Cut 2 of the 2-1/2-inch wide **BLACK** top/bottom inner border strips to this length. Sew the strips to the top/bottom edge of the quilt; press.

Outer Border

Note: *The yardage given allows for the outer border strips to be cut on the lengthwise grain (a couple extra inches are allowed for trimming). Cutting the strips on the lengthwise grain will eliminate the need for piecing or matching the* **PLAID** *outer border strips.*

Cutting

From **GREEN PLAID**:
• Cut 2, 7-1/2 x 80-inch side outer border strips
• Cut 2, 7-1/2 x 62-inch top/bottom outer border strips

From **GREEN PRINT**:
• Cut 1, 7-1/2 x 42-inch strip. From the strip cut: 4, 7-1/2-inch corner squares

Attaching the Border

Step 1   Attach the 7-1/2 x 62-inch **GREEN PLAID** top/bottom outer border strips. Trim the strips as needed.

Step 2   For the side outer borders, measure the quilt from top to bottom, including the seam allowances but not the borders just added. Trim the 7-1/2 x 80-inch **GREEN PLAID** outer border strips to this length. Sew the 7-1/2-inch **GREEN** corner squares to both ends of the side border strips; press. Sew the border strips to the side edges of the quilt; press.

Putting It All Together

Cut the 5-5/8 yard length of backing fabric in half crosswise to make 2, 2-3/4 yard lengths. Refer to **Finishing the Quilt** on page 215 for complete instructions.

Binding

Cutting

From **RED PRINT**:
• Cut 9, 2-3/4 x 42-inch strips

Sew the binding to the quilt using a 3/8-inch seam allowance. This measurement will produce a 1/2-inch wide finished double binding. Refer to **Binding and Diagonal Piecing** on page 215 for complete instructions.

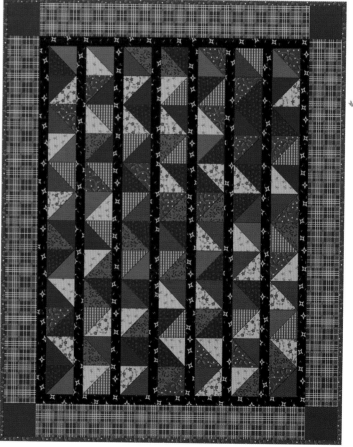

Northern Lights
72 x 90-inches

December Tree

Pillow

16-inches square without ruffle

Fabrics & Supplies

1/4 yard **BEIGE PRINT** for background

1/4 yard **GREEN PRINT** for tree

3/8 yard **RED PRINT** for tree base and inner ruffle

5/8 yard **TAN PRINT** for border and pillow back

3/8 yard **GREEN PLAID** for outer ruffle

18-inch square **BEIGE PRINT**
for quilted pillow lining

quilt batting, at least 18-inches square

16-inch pillow form

Before beginning this project,
read through **Getting Started** on page 210.

Pillow Top

Cutting

From **BEIGE PRINT:**
- Cut 2, 4-1/2 x 6-1/2-inch rectangles
- Cut 2, 4-1/2-inch squares
- Cut 2, 2-1/2-inch squares
- Cut 2, 2-1/2 x 4-1/2-inch rectangles

From **GREEN PRINT:**
- Cut 1, 4-1/2 x 8-1/2-inch rectangle
- Cut 1, 4-1/2 x 12-1/2-inch rectangle
- Cut 1, 2-1/2 x 12-1/2-inch rectangle

From **RED PRINT:**
- Cut 1, 2-1/2 x 8-1/2-inch rectangle

From **TAN PRINT:**
- Cut 2, 2-1/2 x 42-inch strips. From the strips cut:
  2, 2-1/2 x 12-1/2-inch border strips
  2, 2-1/2 x 16-1/2-inch border strips

Piecing

Step 1   With right sides together, position a
4-1/2 x 6-1/2-inch **BEIGE** rectangle on the corner
of the 4-1/2 x 8-1/2-inch **GREEN** rectangle. Draw
a diagonal line on the rectangle and sew on the
line. Trim the seam allowance to 1/4-inch; press.
Repeat this process at the opposite corner of the
rectangle. <u>At this point the tree top unit should
measure 4-1/2 x 12-1/2-inches.</u>

Make 1

Step 2 With right sides together, position the 4-1/2-inch **BEIGE** squares on the corners of the 4-1/2 x 12-1/2-inch **GREEN** rectangle. Draw a diagonal line on the squares; stitch, trim, and press. At this point the unit should measure 4-1/2 x 12-1/2-inches.

Make 1

Step 3 With right sides together, position the 2-1/2-inch **BEIGE** squares on the corners of the 2-1/2 x 12-1/2-inch **GREEN** rectangle. Draw a diagonal line on the squares; stitch, trim, and press. At this point the unit should measure 2-1/2 x 12-1/2-inches.

Make 1

Step 4 With right sides together, position the 2-1/2 x 4-1/2-inch **BEIGE** rectangles on the corners of the 2-1/2 x 8-1/2-inch **RED** rectangle. Draw a diagonal line on the **BEIGE** rectangles; stitch, trim, and press. At this point the unit should measure 2-1/2 x 12-1/2-inches.

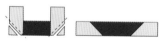
Make 1

Step 5 Sew together the Step 1 through 4 units; press. At this point the tree block should measure 12-1/2-inches square.

Step 6 Sew the 2-1/2 x 12-1/2-inch **TAN** border strips to the top/bottom edges of the tree block; press. Sew the 2-1/2 x 16-1/2-inch **TAN** border strips to the side edges of the tree block; press.

Putting It All Together

Step 1 Layer the pillow top, quilt batting square, and the **BEIGE** lining square with right sides facing out. Hand baste the layers together and quilt as desired.

Step 2 To prepare the pillow top before attaching the ruffle, I suggest hand basting the edges of the 3 layers together. This will prevent the edge of the pillow top from rippling when the ruffle is attached.

Pillow Ruffle

Note: By sewing 2 different width fabrics together, you form the illusion of a double ruffle without all the additional bulk.

Cutting

From **RED PRINT:**
• Cut 4, 2-1/2 x 42-inch inner ruffle strips

From **GREEN PLAID:**
• Cut enough 3-inch wide **bias** strips to measure 170-inches long for the outer ruffle strips

Piecing and Attaching the Ruffle

Step 1 Diagonally piece together the 2-1/2-inch wide **RED** strips.

Step 2 Diagonally piece together the 3-inch wide **GREEN PLAID** strips.

Step 3 Aligning long edges, sew together the **RED** and **GREEN PLAID** strips; press.

Step 4 Diagonally piece the **RED/GREEN PLAID** strips together to make a continuous ruffle strip. Fold the strip in half lengthwise, wrong sides together; press. Divide the ruffle strip into 4 equal segments; mark the quarter points with safety pins.

Step 5 To gather the ruffle, position quilting thread (or pearl cotton) 1/4-inch from the raw edges of the folded ruffle strip. You will need a length of thread 130-inches long. Secure one end of the thread by stitching across it. Zigzag stitch over the thread all the way around the ruffle strip, taking care not to sew through it.

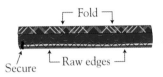

Step 6 Divide the edges of the pillow top into 4 equal segments and mark the quarter points with safety pins. With right sides together and raw edges aligned, pin the ruffle to the pillow top, matching the quarter points. Gently pull up the gathering stitches until the ruffle fits the pillow top, taking care to allow a little extra fullness in the ruffle at each corner. Sew the ruffle to the pillow top, using a 1/4-inch seam allowance.

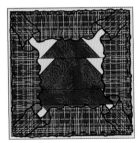

Pillow Back

Cutting

From **TAN PRINT**:
• Cut 2, 16-1/2 x 20-inch rectangles

Assemble the Pillow Back

Step 1 With wrong sides together, fold each 16-1/2 x 20-inch **TAN** rectangle in half crosswise to make 2, 10 x 16-1/2-inch double thick pillow back pieces. Overlap the 2 folded edges by about 4-inches so that the pillow back measures 16-1/2-inches square; pin. Stitch around the entire pillow piece to create a single pillow back, using a scant 1/4-inch seam allowance. The double thickness of each pillow back piece will make the pillow more stable and give it a nice finishing touch.

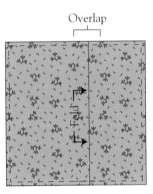

Step 2 With right sides together, layer the pillow back and the pillow top; pin. The ruffle will be sandwiched between the 2 layers and turned toward the center of the pillow at this time. Pin and stitch around the outside edges using a 3/8-inch seam allowance.

Step 3 Turn the pillow right side out, insert the pillow form through the back opening, and fluff up the ruffle.

Courthouse Steps

The balanced geometry of the
Courthouse Steps creates a visually
pleasing and calming quiet. A touch of
plaid in the sashing strips adds a little
spark and contrast to the abundance of
prints used for the Log Cabin blocks.

Courthouse Steps

74 x 94-inches

Fabrics & Supplies

1/8 yard **CHESTNUT/RED PLAID**
for center squares

1/8 yard **BEIGE PRINT #1** for blocks

1/4 yard *each* **GOLD FLORAL**
and **BEIGE PRINT #2** for blocks

1/2 yard *each* **BEIGE FLORAL**
and **TAN PRINT** for blocks

2-7/8 yards **LARGE GOLD FLORAL**
for blocks and outer border

1/4 yard **GREEN FLORAL** for blocks

3/8 yard *each* **BEIGE PRINT #3, BROWN
GRID,** and **GREEN PRINT #1** for blocks

1/2 yard *each* **RED PRINT** and **EGGPLANT
PRINT** for blocks

3/4 yard **GREEN PRINT #2**
for blocks and lattice posts

1 yard **BROWN PRINT** for blocks

1-3/8 yards **GREEN/TAN PLAID**
for lattice strips

1-7/8 yards **GREEN/TAN PLAID**
for binding (cut on bias)

5-3/4 yards backing fabric

quilt batting, at least 80 x 100-inches

Before beginning this project,
read through **Getting Started** on page 210.

Courthouse Steps Blocks

Makes 12 blocks

Cutting

From **CHESTNUT/RED PLAID:**
• Cut 1, 2-1/2 x 42-inch strip.
  From the strip cut:
  12, 2-1/2-inch center squares

From **BEIGE PRINT #1** for position #1:
• Cut 2, 1-1/2 x 42-inch strips

From **GOLD FLORAL** for position #2:
• Cut 3, 1-1/2 x 42-inch strips

From **BEIGE PRINT #2** for position #3:
• Cut 5, 1-1/2 x 42-inch strips

From **BEIGE PRINT #3** for position #4:
• Cut 6, 1-1/2 x 42-inch strips

From **BEIGE FLORAL** for position #5:
• Cut 8, 1-1/2 x 42-inch strips

From **TAN PRINT** for position #6:
• Cut 8, 1-1/2 x 42-inch strips

From **LARGE GOLD FLORAL** for position #7:
• Cut 12, 2-1/2 x 42-inch strips

From **GREEN FLORAL** for position #8:
• Cut 3, 1-1/2 x 42-inch strips

From **BROWN GRID** for position #9:
• Cut 4, 1-1/2 x 42-inch strips

From **GREEN PRINT #1** for position #10:
• Cut 6, 1-1/2 x 42-inch strips

From **RED PRINT** for position #11:
• Cut 8, 1-1/2 x 42-inch strips

From **EGGPLANT PRINT** for position #12:
• Cut 8, 1-1/2 x 42-inch strips

From **GREEN PRINT #2** for position #13:
• Cut 12, 1-1/2 x 42-inch strips

From **BROWN PRINT** for position #14:
• Cut 12, 2-1/2 x 42-inch strips

Piecing

Step 1   Sew a 1-1/2-inch wide **BEIGE PRINT #1** strip to the top/bottom edges of a 2-1/2-inch **CHESTNUT/RED PLAID** center square. Press the seam allowance toward the strips just added and trim the strips even with the edges of the square.

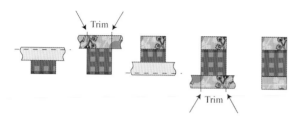

Step 2   Sew a 1-1/2-inch wide **GREEN FLORAL** strip to both side edges of the unit; press and trim.

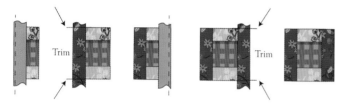

Step 3   Continue sewing the 1-1/2-inch wide *light* strips to the top/bottom edges of the unit, and sew the 1-1/2-inch wide *dark* strips to the side edges of the unit, referring to the block diagram for color placement. Press the seam allowances toward the strips and trim before adding the next. Sew 2-1/2-inch wide **LARGE GOLD FLORAL** strips to the top/bottom edges of the block and sew 2-1/2-inch wide **BROWN PRINT** strips to the side edges of the block; press and trim. At this point each Courthouse Steps block should measure 18-1/2-inches square.

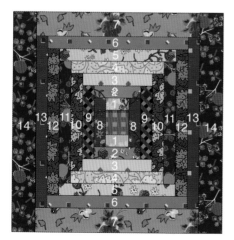

Make 12

Quilt Center

Note: *The yardage given allows for the lattice post squares and lattice segments to be cut on the crosswise grain. Diagonally piece the strips as needed, referring to* **Diagonal Piecing** *instructions on page 215.*

Cutting

From **GREEN/TAN PLAID:**
- Cut 16, 2-1/2 x 42-inch strips.
    From the strips cut:
    31, 2-1/2 x 18-1/2-inch lattice segments

From **GREEN PRINT #2:**
- Cut 2, 2-1/2 x 42-inch strips.
    From the strips cut:
    20, 2-1/2-inch lattice post squares

Quilt Center Assembling

Step 1   Referring to the quilt diagram for placement, sew together 4 of the 2-1/2 x 18-1/2-inch **GREEN/TAN PLAID** lattice segments and 3 Courthouse Steps blocks; press. Make 4 block rows. At this point each block row should measure 18-1/2 x 62-1/2-inches.

Step 2   Referring to the quilt diagram, sew together 3 of the 2-1/2 x 18-1/2-inch **GREEN/TAN PLAID** lattice segments and 4 of the 2-1/2-inch **GREEN PRINT #2** lattice post squares; press. Make 5 lattice strips. At this point each lattice strip should measure 2-1/2 x 62-1/2-inches.

Step 3   Pin the block rows and the lattice strips together at the block intersections. Sew the strips together; press the seam allowances in one direction.

Outer Border

Note: *The yardage given allows for the border strips to be cut on the crosswise grain. Diagonally piece the strips as needed, referring to* **Diagonal Piecing** *instructions on page 215. Read through* **Border** *instructions on page 214 for general instructions on adding borders.*

Cutting

From **LARGE GOLD FLORAL:**
- Cut 10, 6-1/2 x 42-inch outer border strips

Attaching the Border

Attach the 6-1/2-inch wide **LARGE GOLD FLORAL** outer border.

Putting It All Together

Cut the 5-3/4 yard length of backing fabric in half crosswise to make 2, 2-7/8 yard lengths. Refer to **Finishing the Quilt** on page 215 for complete instructions.

Binding

Cutting

From **GREEN/TAN PLAID:**
- Cut enough 6-1/2-inch wide **bias** strips to make a 350-inch long strip.

Sew the binding to the quilt using a 1-inch seam allowance. This measurement will produce a 1-inch wide finished double binding. Refer to **Binding and Diagonal Piecing** on page 215 for complete instructions.

Courthouse Steps

74 x 94-inches

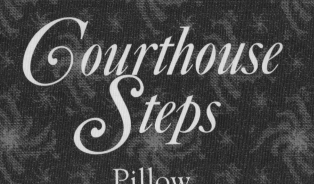

Courthouse Steps
Pillow

18-inches square

1/8 yard **CHESTNUT/RED PLAID**
for center square

1/8 yard *each* **BEIGE PRINT #1, #2, #3,**
and **BEIGE FLORAL** for block

1/8 yard *each* **GOLD FLORAL, TAN PRINT,**
and **LARGE GOLD FLORAL** for block

1/8 yard *each* **GREEN FLORAL** and **GREEN
PRINT #2** for block

7/8 yard **GREEN PRINT #1** for block and ruffle

1/8 yard *each* **BROWN GRID**
and **BROWN PRINT** for block

1/8 yard **EGGPLANT PRINT** for block

3/4 yard **RED PRINT** for block and pillow back

18-inch square pillow form

Before beginning this project,
read through **Getting Started** on page 210.

Courthouse Steps Block

Makes 1 block

Cutting

From **CHESTNUT/RED PLAID:**
• Cut 1, 2-1/2-inch center square

From **BEIGE PRINT #1** for position #1:
• Cut 1, 1-1/2 x 42-inch strip

From **GOLD FLORAL** for position #2:
• Cut 1, 1-1/2 x 42-inch strip

From **BEIGE PRINT #2** for position #3:
• Cut 1, 1-1/2 x 42-inch strip

From **BEIGE PRINT #3** for position #4:
• Cut 1, 1-1/2 x 42-inch strip

From **BEIGE FLORAL** for position #5:
• Cut 1, 1-1/2 x 42-inch strip

From **TAN PRINT** for position #6:
• Cut 1, 1-1/2 x 42-inch strip

From **LARGE GOLD FLORAL** for position #7:
• Cut 1, 2-1/2 x 42-inch strip

From **GREEN FLORAL** for position #8:
• Cut 1, 1-1/2 x 42-inch strip

From **BROWN GRID** for position #9:
• Cut 1, 1-1/2 x 42-inch strip

From **GREEN PRINT #1** for position #10:
• Cut 1, 1-1/2 x 42-inch strip

From **RED PRINT** for position #11:
• Cut 1, 1-1/2 x 42-inch strip

From **EGGPLANT PRINT** for position #12:
• Cut 1, 1-1/2 x 42-inch strip

From **GREEN PRINT #2** for position #13:
• Cut 1, 1-1/2 x 42-inch strip

From **BROWN PRINT** for position #14:
• Cut 1, 2-1/2 x 42-inch strip

Piecing

Make 1 Courthouse Steps block referring to
Courthouse Steps Quilt instructions and diagrams,
Steps 1 through 3 on page 155.

Pillow Ruffle

Cutting

From **GREEN PRINT #1:**
• Cut 5, 4-1/2 x 42-inch strips

Attaching the Ruffle

Step 1   Diagonally piece the 4-1/2-inch wide **GREEN PRINT #1** strips together to make a continuous ruffle strip, referring to **Diagonal Piecing** instructions on page 215. Fold the strip in half lengthwise, wrong sides together; press. Divide the ruffle strip into 4 equal segments; mark the quarter points with safety pins.

Step 2   To gather the ruffle, position quilting thread (or pearl cotton) 1/4-inch from the raw edges of the folded ruffle strip. You will need a length of thread 144-inches long. Secure one end of thread by stitching across it. Zigzag stitch over the thread all the way around the ruffle strip, taking care not to sew through it.

Step 3   Divide the edges of the pillow top into 4 equal segments and mark quarter points with safety pins. With right sides together and raw edges aligned, pin the ruffle to the pillow top, matching the quarter points. Pull up the gathering stitches until the ruffle fits the pillow top, taking care to allow fullness in the ruffle at each corner. Sew the ruffle to the pillow top, using a scant 1/4-inch seam allowance.

Pillow Back

Cutting

From **RED PRINT:**
• Cut 2, 18-1/2 x 22-inch rectangles

Pillow Back Assembly

Step 1   With wrong sides together, fold each 2, 18-1/2 x 22-inch rectangle in half to make 2, 11 x 18-1/2-inch double-thick pillow back pieces.

Step 2   Overlap the 2 folded edges by about 4-inches so that the pillow back measures 18-1/2-inches square; pin. Machine baste around the entire piece to create a single pillow back, using a 1/4-inch seam allowance. The double thickness of the pillow back will make it more stable and give it a nice finishing touch.

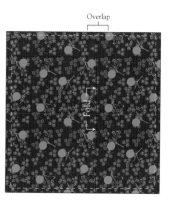

Step 3   With right sides together, layer the pillow back and the pillow top; pin. The ruffle will be sandwiched between the 2 layers and turned toward the center of the pillow at this time. Stitch around the outside edges using a 3/8-inch seam allowance. Turn the pillow right side out and fluff up the ruffle. Insert the pillow form through the back opening.

Courthouse Steps Pillow 18-inches square without ruffle

Winter Bright
Throw

Deep red, green, and gold strike it rich in this graphic Winter Bright tribute to holiday-themed decorating. The center twist in each of the all-over repeated patchwork blocks adds interest and a dramatic sense of movement.

Winter Bright

Throw

68 x 77-inches

Fabrics & Supplies

1-1/8 yards **GREEN DOT** for blocks

1 yard **GREEN PRINT** for blocks and lattice posts

2-3/8 yards **BEIGE PRINT**
for blocks and outer border

1-1/4 yards **GOLD PRINT** for blocks

1-7/8 yards **RED PRINT**
for lattice pieces and inner border

3/4 yard **GREEN DOT** for binding

4 yards backing fabric

quilt batting, at least 74 x 83-inches

Before beginning this project,
read through **Getting Started** on page 210.

Pieced Blocks

Makes 42 blocks

Cutting

From **GREEN DOT:**
- Cut 8, 2-1/2 x 42-inch strips. From the strips cut:
  84, 2-1/2 x 3-1/2-inch rectangles
- Cut 10, 1-1/2 x 42-inch strips.
  From the strips cut:
  252, 1-1/2-inch squares

From **GREEN PRINT:**
- Cut 4, 2-7/8 x 42-inch strips
- Cut 9, 1-1/2 x 42-inch strips. From the strips cut:
  42, 1-1/2 x 5-1/2-inch rectangles
  84, 1-1/2-inch squares

From **BEIGE PRINT:**
- Cut 4, 2-7/8 x 42-inch strips
- Cut 6, 2-1/2 x 42-inch strips. From the strips cut:
  84, 2-1/2-inch squares

From **GOLD PRINT:**
- Cut 26, 1-1/2 x 42-inch strips. From the strips cut:
  168, 1-1/2 x 3-1/2-inch rectangles
  168, 1-1/2 x 2-1/2-inch rectangles

Piecing

Step 1 With right sides together, position
a 2-1/2-inch **BEIGE** square on the corner of a
2-1/2 x 3-1/2-inch **GREEN DOT** rectangle. Draw a
diagonal line on the square and stitch on the line.
Trim the seam allowance to 1/4-inch; press.

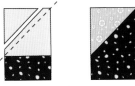

Make 84

Step 2 With right sides together, layer the
2-7/8 x 42-inch **BEIGE** and **GREEN PRINT** strips
together in pairs. Press together, but do not sew. Cut

the layered strips into squares. Cut the layered squares in half diagonally to make 84 sets of triangles. Stitch 1/4-inch from the diagonal edge of each pair of triangles; press.

Crosscut 42, 2-7/8-inch squares

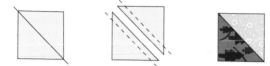

Make 84, 2-1/2-inch triangle-pieced squares

Step 3   Sew the Step 1 and Step 2 units together in pairs; press. Make 84 units. Sew the units to both long edges of the 1-1/2 x 5-1/2-inch **GREEN PRINT** rectangles; press. At this point each unit should measure 5-1/2-inches square.

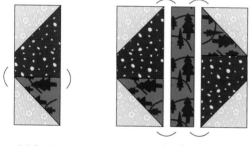

Make 84   Make 42

Step 4   With right sides together, position a 1-1/2-inch **GREEN PRINT** square on the left corner of a 1-1/2 x 3-1/2-inch **GOLD** rectangle. Draw a diagonal line on the square; stitch, trim, and press. Sew a 1-1/2 x 2-1/2-inch **GOLD** rectangle to the left edge of the unit; press. At this point each unit should measure 1-1/2 x 5-1/2-inches. Referring to the block diagram, sew the units to the top/bottom edges of the pieced block; press.

Make 84

Step 5   With right sides together, position a 1-1/2-inch **GREEN DOT** square on the left corner of a 1-1/2 x 3-1/2-inch **GOLD** rectangle. Draw a diagonal line on the square; stitch, trim, and press.

Sew a 1-1/2 x 2-1/2-inch **GOLD** rectangle to the left edge of the unit; press. Sew 1-1/2-inch **GREEN DOT** squares to both edges of the unit; press. At this point each unit should measure 1-1/2 x 7-1/2-inches. Referring to the block diagram, sew the units to the side edges of the pieced block; press. At this point each pieced block should measure 7-1/2-inches square.

Make 84

Make 42

Quilt Center

Cutting

From **RED PRINT:**
- Cut 15, 2-1/2 x 42-inch strips.
   From the strips cut:
   71, 2-1/2 x 7-1/2-inch lattice segments

From **GREEN PRINT:**
- Cut 2, 2-1/2 x 42-inch strips.
   From the strips cut:
   30, 2-1/2-inch lattice post squares

Quilt Center Assembly

Step 1   Sew together 6 of the pieced blocks and 5 of the 2-1/2 x 7-1/2-inch **RED** lattice segments. Press the seam allowances toward the lattice segments. Make 7 block rows. At this point each block row should measure 7-1/2 x 52-1/2-inches.

Step 2   Sew together 5 of the 2-1/2-inch **GREEN PRINT** lattice posts and 6 of the 2-1/2 x 7-1/2-inch **RED** lattice segments. Press the seam allowances toward the lattice segments. Make 6 lattice strips. <u>At this point each lattice strip should measure 2-1/2 x 52-1/2-inches.</u>

Step 3   Pin the block rows and the lattice strips together at the block intersections and sew. Press the seam allowances toward the lattice strips.

Borders

Note: *The yardage given allows for the border strips to be cut on the crosswise grain. Diagonally piece the strips as needed, referring to* **Diagonal Piecing** *instructions on page 215. Read through* **Border** *instructions on page 214 for general instructions on adding borders.*

Cutting

From **RED PRINT:**
• Cut 8, 2-1/2 x 42-inch inner border strips

From **BEIGE PRINT:**
• Cut 8, 6-1/2 x 42-inch outer border strips

Attaching the Borders

Step 1   Attach the 2-1/2-inch wide **RED** inner border strips.

Step 2   Attach the 6-1/2-inch wide **BEIGE** outer border strips.

Putting It All Together

Cut the 4 yard length of backing fabric in half crosswise to make 2, 2 yard lengths. Refer to **Finishing the Quilt** on page 215 for complete instructions.

Binding

Cutting

From **RED PRINT:**
• Cut 8, 2-3/4 x 42-inch strips

Sew the binding to the quilt using a 3/8-inch seam allowance. This measurement will produce a 1/2-inch wide finished double binding. Refer to **Binding and Diagonal Piecing** instructions on page 215 for complete instructions.

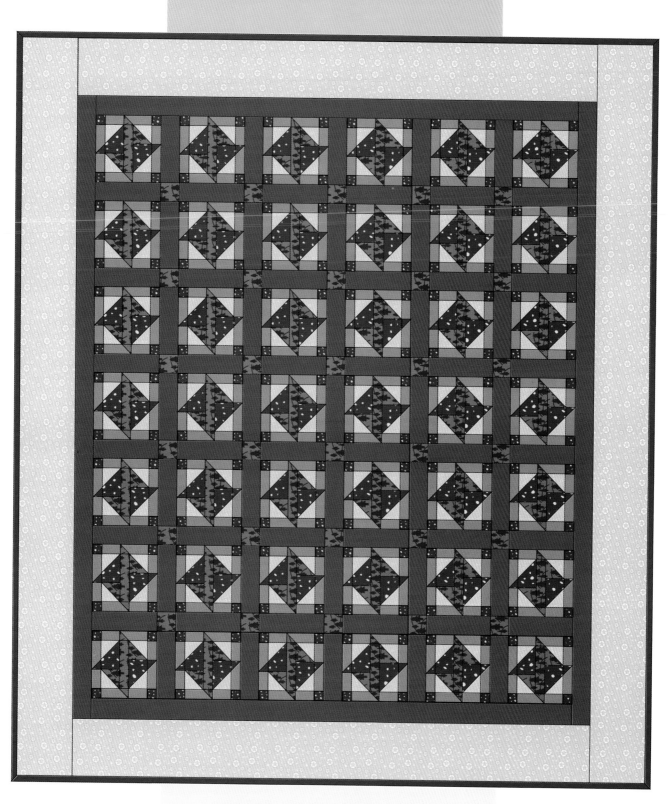

Winter Bright
Throw
68 x 77-inches

Leaf Gathering

The glories of autumn come home with
one simple, but spectacular leaf-filled
quilt. The multitude of colors represents
the layering of leaves in bright hues of
brown, green, gold, and red, combined
with the warm afternoon sun and cool
nights filled with twinkling stars.

Leaf Gathering

74 x 86-inches

Fabrics & Supplies

2-3/4 yards **BEIGE PRINT** for background

5/8 yard **GOLD PRINT** for star blocks

1-1/4 yards **EGGPLANT PRINT**
for nine-patch blocks, inner border,
and narrow middle border

1/4 yard *each* of **4 ORANGE** and **CHESTNUT
PRINTS** for nine-patch blocks

1/4 yard *each* of **2 RED PRINTS**
for nine-patch blocks

1/8 yard *each* of **4 GOLD, BROWN,** and **RED
PRINTS** for nine-patch blocks

1/3 yard *each* of **5 GREEN PRINTS**
for leaf blocks

7/8 yard **BROWN PRINT**
for wide middle border

1-1/2 yards **LARGE GREEN FLORAL**
for outer border

7/8 yard **BROWN PRINT** for binding

5-1/4 yards backing fabric

quilt batting, at least 80 x 92-inches

Before beginning this project,
read through **Getting Started** on page 210.

Star Blocks

Makes 19 blocks

Cutting

From **BEIGE PRINT:**
- Cut 5, 2-1/2 x 42-inch strips. From the strips cut:
    38, 2-1/2 x 4-1/2-inch rectangles
- Cut 5 more 2-1/2 x 42-inch strips.
    From the strips cut:
    76, 2-1/2-inch squares

From **GOLD PRINT:**
- Cut 4, 2-1/2 x 42-inch strips. From the strips cut:
    19, 2-1/2 x 6-1/2-inch rectangles
- Cut 3 more 2-1/2 x 42-inch strips.
    From the strips cut:
    38, 2-1/2-inch squares

Piecing

Step 1   With right sides together, position
2-1/2-inch **BEIGE** squares on both corners of a
2-1/2 x 6-1/2-inch **GOLD** rectangle. Draw a diagonal
line on the squares, and stitch on the lines. Trim the
seam allowances to 1/4-inch; press.

Make 19

Step 2   With right sides together, position a
2-1/2-inch **GOLD** square on the right corner of a
2-1/2 x 4-1/2-inch **BEIGE** rectangle. Draw a diagonal
line on the square; stitch, trim, and press. Sew a
2-1/2-inch **BEIGE** square to the right edge of the
unit; press.

Make 38

Step 3   Sew Step 2 units to the top/bottom edges of
a Step 1 unit; press. <u>At this point each star block
should measure 6-1/2-inches square.</u>

Make 19

Nine-Patch Blocks

Makes 50 blocks

Cutting

From **BEIGE PRINT**:
• Cut 16, 2-1/2 x 42-inch strips

From **EGGPLANT PRINT**:
• Cut 4, 2-1/2 x 42-inch strips

From *each* **ORANGE** and **CHESTNUT PRINT**:
• Cut 2, 2-1/2 x 42-inch strips

From *each* **RED PRINT**:
• Cut 2, 2-1/2 x 42-inch strips

From *each* **GOLD**, **BROWN**, and **RED PRINT**:
• Cut 1, 2-1/2 x 42-inch strip

Piecing

Step 1 Aligning long edges, sew a 2-1/2 x 42-inch **BEIGE** strip to both side edges of a 2-1/2 x 42-inch **EGGPLANT** strip; press. Make 4 strip sets. Cut the strip sets into segments.

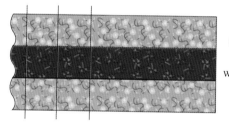

Crosscut 50, 2-1/2-inch wide segments

Step 2 Aligning long edges, sew a 2-1/2 x 42-inch **ORANGE** or **CHESTNUT** strip to one edge of a 2-1/2 x 42-inch **BEIGE** strip; press. In the same manner, sew a **RED**, **GOLD**, or **BROWN** strip to the opposite edge of the unit; press. Make 8 strip sets using the remaining **ORANGE** and **CHESTNUT** strips and the remaining **RED**, **GOLD**, and **BROWN** strips. Cut the strip sets into segments.

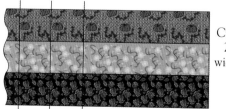

Crosscut 100, 2-1/2-inch wide segments

Step 3 Sew Step 2 units to both side edges of a Step 1 unit; press. At this point each nine-patch block should measure 6-1/2-inches square.

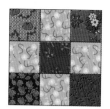

Make 50

Leaf Blocks

Makes 30 blocks

Cutting

From *each* **ASSORTED GREEN PRINT**:
• Cut 1, 4-1/2 x 42-inch strip. From the strip cut:
  6, 4-1/2-inch squares
• Cut 2, 2-1/2 x 42-inch strips. From the strips cut:
  12, 2-1/2 x 4-1/2-inch rectangles
• Cut 1, 1 x 42-inch strip. From the strip cut:
  6, 1 x 5-inch strips

From **BEIGE PRINT**:
• Cut 2, 2-5/8 x 42-inch strips. From the strips cut:
  30, 2-5/8-inch squares
• Cut 8, 2-1/2 x 42-inch strips. From the strips cut:
  120, 2-1/2-inch squares

Piecing

Step 1 With right sides together, position 2-1/2-inch **BEIGE** squares on 2 opposite corners of a 4-1/2-inch **GREEN** square. Draw a diagonal line on the squares; stitch, trim, and press.

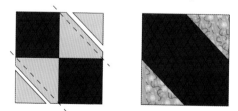

Make 6 from each **GREEN PRINT**

Step 2 With right sides together, position a 2-1/2-inch **BEIGE** square on the right corner of a 2-1/2 x 4-1/2-inch **GREEN** rectangle. Draw a diagonal line on the square; stitch, trim, and press.

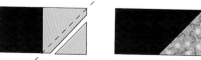

Make 6 from each **GREEN PRINT**

Step 3 Repeat Step 2, reversing the direction of the stitching line.

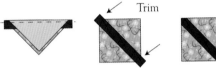

Make 6 from each **GREEN PRINT**

Step 4 To make the stem unit, cut the 2-5/8-inch **BEIGE** squares in half diagonally. Center a **BEIGE** triangle on a 1 x 5-inch **GREEN** strip; stitch a 1/4-inch seam. Center another **BEIGE** triangle on the opposite edge of the **GREEN** strip; stitch. Press the seam allowances toward the **GREEN** strip. Trim the stem unit so it measures 2-1/2-inches square.

Trim

Make 6 from each **GREEN PRINT**

Step 5 Referring to the block diagram, lay out the units from Steps 1 through 4 in horizontal rows. Sew the rows together to complete the leaf block; press. <u>At this point each block should measure 6-1/2-inches square.</u>

Make 6 from each
GREEN PRINT
for a total of 30

Quilt Center

Step 1 Referring to the quilt diagram for block placement, sew the blocks together in 11 horizontal rows of 9 blocks each. Press the seam allowance in alternating directions by rows so the seams will fit snugly together with less bulk.

Step 2 Pin the rows at the block intersections; sew together. Press the seam allowances in one direction. <u>At this point the quilt center should measure 54-1/2 x 66-1/2-inches.</u>

Borders

Note: *The yardage given allows for the border strips to be cut on the crosswise grain. Diagonally piece the strips*

*as needed, referring to **Diagonal Piecing** instructions on page 215. Read through **Border** instructions on page 214 for general instructions on adding borders.*

Cutting

From **EGGPLANT PRINT:**
- Cut 7, 1-1/2 x 42-inch inner border strips
- Cut 8, 1-1/2 x 42-inch narrow middle border strips

From **BROWN PRINT:**
- Cut 7, 3-1/2 x 42-inch wide middle border strips

From **LARGE GREEN FLORAL:**
- Cut 9, 5-1/2 x 42-inch outer border strips

Attaching the Borders

Step 1 Attach the 1-1/2-inch wide **EGGPLANT** inner border strips.

Step 2 Attach the 3-1/2-inch wide **BROWN** wide middle border strips.

Step 3 Attach the 1-1/2-inch wide **EGGPLANT** narrow middle border strips.

Step 4 Attach the 5-1/2-inch wide **LARGE GREEN FLORAL** outer border strips.

Putting It All Together

Cut the 5-1/4 yard length of backing fabric in half crosswise to make 2, 2-5/8 yard lengths. Refer to **Finishing the Quilt** on page 215 for complete instructions.

Binding

Cutting

From **BROWN PRINT:**
- Cut 9, 2-3/4 x 42-inch strips

Sew the binding to the quilt using a 3/8-inch seam allowance. This measurement will produce a 1/2-inch wide finished double binding. Refer to **Binding and Diagonal Piecing** on page 215 for complete instructions.

Leaf Gathering
74 x 86-inches

Block Party

Treat yourself or guests to a quilt that is
quick to make, easy to love, and just the
right size for lazy Sunday afternoon naps.
Throw your own Block Party with
stenciled boxes—each filled with a
block's worth of fabrics for guests to take
home as a memorable party favor.

Block Party

72 x 80-inches

Fabrics & Supplies

1-5/8 yards **BLUE PRINT**
for blocks and pieced border

1/8 yard **SOLID BLUE** for blocks

1-5/8 yards **GREEN PRINT**
for blocks and pieced border

1/8 yard **SOLID GREEN** for blocks

1 yard **PINK PRINT** for blocks

1/8 yard **SOLID PINK** for blocks

3-7/8 yards **BEIGE PRINT**
for blocks and borders

7/8 yard **BLUE PRINT** for binding

4-3/4 yards backing fabric

quilt batting, at least 78 x 86-inches

Before beginning this project,
read through **Getting Started** on page 210.

Pieced Blocks

Makes 14 blocks from each of the 3 color combinations

Cutting

From **BLUE, GREEN,** and **PINK PRINTS:**
- Cut 11, 2-1/2 x 42-inch strips from *each* fabric.
    From the strips cut:
    28, 2-1/2 x 8-1/2-inch rectangles
    28, 2-1/2 x 4-1/2-inch rectangles

From **BLUE, GREEN,** and **PINK SOLIDS:**
- Cut 1, 2-1/2 x 42-inch strip from *each* fabric

From **BEIGE PRINT:**
- Cut 16, 1-1/2 x 42-inch strips.
    From 10 of the strips cut:
    84, 1-1/2 x 4-1/2-inch rectangles. The
    remaining 6 strips will be used in the
    Step 1 and 2 strip sets.

Piecing

Step 1   Aligning long raw edges, sew
1-1/2 x 42-inch **BEIGE** strips to both side
edges of the 2-1/2 x 42-inch **SOLID BLUE** strip;
press. Press the strip set, referring to **Hints and Helps
on Pressing Strip Sets** on page 214. Cut the strip set
into segments.

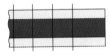

Crosscut 14, 2-1/2-inch segments

Step 2   Repeat Step 1 sewing the 1-1/2 x 42-inch
BEIGE strips to both side edges of the
2-1/2 x 42-inch **SOLID GREEN** and **SOLID PINK**
strips. Cut the strip sets into segments.

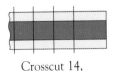

Crosscut 14,
2-1/2-inch segments

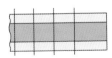

Crosscut 14,
2-1/2-inch segments

Step 3 Sew 1-1/2 x 4-1/2-inch **BEIGE** rectangles to both side edges of the Step 1 and Step 2 segments; press. Make 14 units of each of the 3 color combinations.

Make 42

Step 4 Sew 2-1/2 x 4-1/2-inch **BLUE PRINT** rectangles to the top/bottom edges of the Step 3 **SOLID BLUE** units; press.

Step 5 Sew 2-1/2 x 8-1/2-inch **BLUE PRINT** rectangles to the side edges of the Step 4 units; press. <u>At this point each block should measure 8-1/2-inches square.</u>

Make 14

Step 6 Repeat Steps 4 and 5 to make the **GREEN PRINT** blocks and **PINK PRINT** blocks.

Make 14   Make 14

Quilt Center

Step 1 Referring to the quilt diagram for color placement, sew together the blocks in 7 rows of 6 blocks each. Press the seam allowances in alternating directions by rows so the seams will fit snugly together with less bulk.

Step 2 Pin the rows together at the block intersections; stitch and press. <u>At this point the quilt center should measure 48-1/2 x 56-1/2-inches.</u>

Borders

Note: *The yardage given allows for the border strips to be cut on the crosswise grain. Diagonally piece the strips as needed, referring to* **Diagonal Piecing** *instructions on page 215. Read through* **Border** *instructions on page 214 for general instructions on adding borders.*

Cutting

From **BEIGE PRINT:**
- Cut 14, 4-1/2 x 42-inch strips for the inner and outer borders
- Cut 8, 4-1/2 x 42-inch strips. From the strips cut:
  30, 4-1/2 x 8-1/2-inch rectangles
  4, 4-1/2-inch squares for the pieced border.

From **BLUE** and **GREEN PRINTS:**
- Cut 4, 4-1/2 x 42-inch strips from *each* fabric. From the strips cut:
  30, 4-1/2-inch squares from *each* fabric.

Attaching the Borders

Step 1 Attach the 4-1/2-inch wide **BEIGE** inner border strips.

Step 2 With right sides together, position a 4-1/2-inch **BLUE** square at the left corner of a 4-1/2 x 8-1/2-inch **BEIGE** rectangle. Draw a diagonal line on the square; stitch, trim, and press. Repeat this process at the opposite corner of the rectangle using a **GREEN** square.

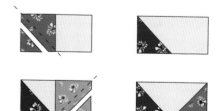

Make 30

Step 3 Referring to the quilt diagram for color placement, sew 7 of the Step 2 units together for the top/bottom borders; press. Sew the border strips to the quilt; press.

Step 4 Referring to the quilt diagram for color placement, sew 8 of the Step 2 units together for each side border; press. Sew 4-1/2-inch **BEIGE** squares to both ends of the border strips; press. Sew the border strips to the quilt; press.

Step 5 Attach the 4-1/2-inch wide **BEIGE** outer border strips.

Putting It All Together

Cut the 4-3/4-yard length of backing fabric in half crosswise to make 2, 2-3/8-yard lengths. Refer to **Finishing the Quilt** on page 215 for complete instructions.

Binding

From **BLUE PRINT:**
• Cut 8, 3 x 42-inch strips

Sew the binding to the quilt using a 3/8-inch seam allowance. This measurement will produce a 1/2-inch finished double binding. Refer to **Binding and Diagonal Piecing** page 215 for complete instructions.

Block Party

72 x 80-inches

Goldenrod Patch

Freshen any room with a tabletop floral
display complete with the garden gate.
Carry the old-fashioned charm throughout
the room with a traditional Goldenrod
Patch quilt topped by an antique
embroidered pillow top newly trimmed
with a one-inch-wide ruffle.

Goldenrod Patch

Blue

88 x 96-inches

Fabrics & Supplies

3-3/8 yards **BLUE DOT PRINT** for pieced blocks, sawtooth units, and outer border

4-1/2 yards **BEIGE PRINT** for background and alternate blocks

1-7/8 yards **GOLD PRINT** for block centers, side and corner triangles, and sawtooth units

1/4 yard **DARK BLUE PRINT** for corner squares

7/8 yard **GOLD PLAID** for binding (cut on the bias)

7-7/8 yard backing fabric

quilt batting, at least 94 x 102-inches

Before beginning this project, read through **Getting Started** on page 210.

Pieced Blocks

Makes 90 blocks

Cutting

From **BLUE DOT PRINT:**
- Cut 15, 2-7/8 x 42-inch strips
- Cut 3, 2-1/2 x 42-inch strips. From the strips cut: 36, 2-1/2-inch squares

From **BEIGE PRINT:**
- Cut 15, 2-7/8 x 42-inch strips
- Cut 12, 2-1/2 x 42-inch strips. From the strips cut: 180, 2-1/2-inch squares

From **GOLD PRINT:**
- Cut 6, 2-1/2 x 42-inch strips. From the strips cut: 90, 2-1/2-inch squares

Piecing

Step 1   With right sides together, layer the 2-7/8 x 42-inch **BLUE DOT** and **BEIGE** strips together in pairs. Press together, but do not sew. Cut the layered strips into squares. Cut the layered squares in half diagonally to make 360 sets of triangles. Stitch 1/4-inch from the diagonal edge of each pair of triangles; press.

Crosscut 180, 2-7/8-inch squares

Make 360, 2-1/2-inch triangle-pieced squares

Step 2   Referring to the block diagram, lay out the 2-1/2-inch **BLUE DOT** squares and Step 1 triangle-pieced squares, along with the 2-1/2-inch **GOLD** and **BEIGE** squares. Sew the squares together in horizontal rows. Press the seam allowances away from the triangle-pieced squares. Sew the rows together; press. <u>At this point each block should measure 6-1/2-inches square.</u>

Make 90 blocks

Quilt Center

Note: The side and corner triangles are larger than necessary and will be trimmed before the border is added.

Cutting

From **BEIGE PRINT:**
- Cut 12, 6-1/2 x 42-inch strips.
  From the strips cut:
  72, 6-1/2-inch alternate block squares

From **GOLD PRINT:**
- Cut 3, 10 x 42-inch strips. From the strips cut:
  9, 10-inch squares. Cut the squares diagonally into quarters to make 36 triangles. You will be using only 34 for side triangles.
- Cut 2, 6-inch squares. Cut the squares in half diagonally to make 4 corner triangles.

Quilt Center Assembly

Step 1 Referring to the quilt diagram, sew the pieced blocks, the alternate blocks, and the side triangles together in diagonal rows. Press the seam allowances in alternating directions by rows so the seams will fit snugly together with less bulk.

Step 2 Pin the rows at the block intersections; sew the rows together. Press the seam allowances in one direction.

Step 3 Sew the corner triangles to the quilt center; press.

Step 4 Trim away the excess fabric from the side and corner triangles, taking care to allow a 1/4-inch seam allowance beyond the corners of each block. Refer to **Trimming the Side and Corner Triangles** on page 212 for complete instructions.

Borders

*Note: The yardage given allows for the border strips to be cut on the crosswise grain. Diagonally piece the strips as needed, referring to **Diagonal Piecing** instructions on page 215. Read through **Border** instructions on page 214 for general instructions on adding borders.*

Cutting

From **BLUE DOT PRINT:**
- Cut 9, 6-1/2 x 42-inch border strips
- Cut 1, 2-7/8 x 42-inch strip for sawtooth units

From **GOLD PRINT:**
- Cut 1, 2-7/8 x 42-inch strip for sawtooth units

From **DARK BLUE PRINT:**
- Cut 4, 6-1/2-inch corner squares

Assembling the Sawtooth Units

Step 1 With right sides together, layer the 2-7/8 x 42-inch **BLUE DOT** and **GOLD** strips together. Press together, but do not sew. Cut the layered strips into squares. Cut the layered squares in half diagonally to make 24 sets of triangles. Stitch 1/4-inch from the diagonal edge of each pair of triangles; press.

Crosscut 12, 2-7/8-inch squares

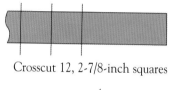

Make 24, 2-1/2-inch triangle-pieced squares

Step 2 Sew 3 of the triangle-pieced squares together for each sawtooth unit; press. <u>At this point each sawtooth unit should measure 2-1/2 x 6-1/2-inches.</u>

Make 4 sawtooth units

Make 4 sawtooth units

Attaching the Border

Step 1 To measure for the 6-1/2-inch wide **BLUE DOT** top/bottom borders, refer to **Border** instructions on page 214. Subtract 4-inches from this measurement to allow for the sawtooth units at each end. Cut 2, 6-1/2-inch wide **BLUE DOT** border strips to this length.

Step 2   Referring to the quilt diagram, sew 2 sawtooth units to each end of the **BLUE DOT** border strips; press. Sew the border strips to the top/bottom edges of the quilt; press.

Step 3   For the side borders, measure the quilt from top to bottom including the seam allowances but not the borders just added. Subtract 4-inches from this measurement to allow for the sawtooth units at each end. Cut 2, 6-1/2-inch wide **BLUE DOT** border strips to this length.

Step 4   Referring to the quilt diagram, sew 2 sawtooth units to each end of the **BLUE DOT** border strips; press. Sew the 6-1/2-inch **DARK BLUE** corner squares to both ends of the border strips; press. Sew the border strips to the side edges of the quilt; press.

Putting It All Together

Cut the 7-7/8 yard length of backing fabric in thirds crosswise to make 3, 2-5/8 yard lengths. Refer to **Finishing the Quilt** on page 215 for complete instructions.

Binding

Cutting

From **GOLD PLAID:**
- Cut enough 2-3/4-inch wide **bias** strips to make a 385-inch long strip

Sew the binding to the quilt using a 3/8-inch seam allowance. This measurement will produce a 1/2-inch wide finished double binding. Refer to **Binding and Diagonal Piecing** instructions on page 215 for complete instructions.

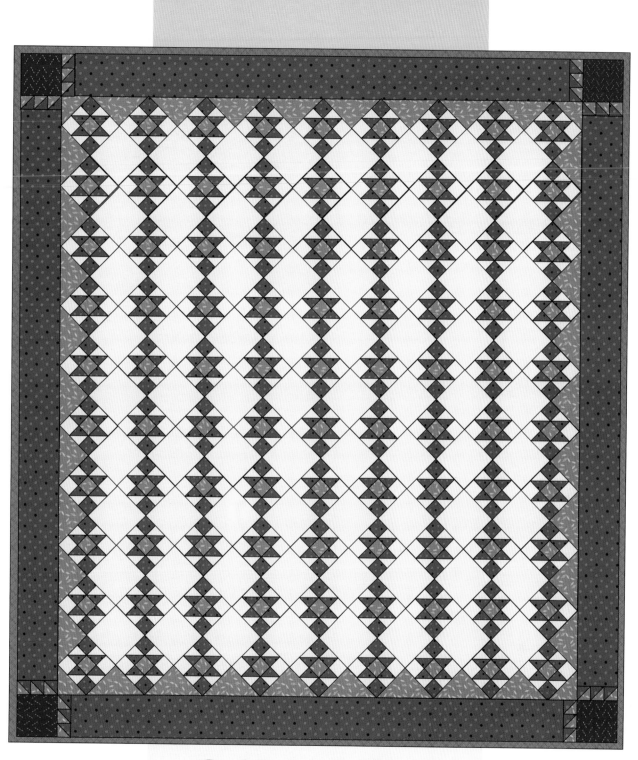

Goldenrod Patch

Blue

88 x 96-inches

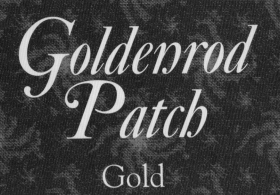

Goldenrod Patch

Gold

88 x 96-inches

Fabrics & Supplies

1-3/4 yards **WINE PRINT** for block centers, side and corner triangles, and sawtooth units

5/8 yard *each* of **5 COORDINATING GOLD PRINTS** for pieced blocks

4-1/2 yards **BEIGE PRINT** or background and alternate blocks

2 yards **WINE FLORAL** for sawtooth units and outer border

1/4 yard **GOLD PLAID** for corner squares

7/8 yard **RUST PLAID** for binding (cut on the bias)

7-7/8 yards backing fabric

quilt batting, at least 94 x 102-inches

Before beginning this project, read through **Getting Started** on page 210.

Pieced Blocks

Makes 90 blocks

Cutting

From *each* of the **5 GOLD PRINTS:**
- Cut 3, 2-7/8 x 42-inch strips
- Cut 3, 2-1/2 x 42-inch strips. From the strips cut: 36, 2-1/2-inch squares

From **BEIGE PRINT:**
- Cut 15, 2-7/8 x 42-inch strips
- Cut 12, 2-1/2 x 42-inch strips. From the strips cut: 180, 2-1/2-inch squares

From **WINE PRINT:**
- Cut 6, 2-1/2 x 42-inch strips. From the strips cut: 90, 2-1/2-inch squares

Piecing

Step 1 With right sides together, layer each of the 2-7/8 x 42-inch **GOLD** strips with a 2-7/8 x 42-inch **BEIGE** strip. Press together, but do not sew. Cut the layered strips into squares. Cut the layered squares in half diagonally to make 72 sets of triangles. Stitch 1/4-inch from the diagonal edge of each pair of triangles; press.

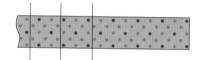

Crosscut 36, 2-7/8-inch squares from *each* GOLD/BEIGE combination

Make 72, 2-1/2-inch triangle-pieced squares from *each* GOLD/BEIGE combination

Step 2 Referring to the block diagram, lay out the coordinating 2-1/2-inch **GOLD** squares and Step 1 triangle-pieced squares, along with the 2-1/2-inch **WINE** and **BEIGE** squares. Sew the squares together in horizontal rows. Press the seam allowances away from the triangle-pieced squares. Sew the rows together; press. At this point each block should measure 6-1/2-inches square.

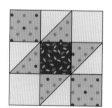

Make 18 blocks from *each* GOLD/BEIGE combination

Quilt Center

Note: *The side and corner triangles are larger than necessary and will be trimmed before the border is added.*

Cutting

From **BEIGE PRINT:**
- Cut 12, 6-1/2 x 42-inch strips. From the strips cut:
    72, 6-1/2-inch alternate block squares

From **WINE PRINT:**
- Cut 3, 10 x 42-inch strips. From the strips cut: 9, 10-inch squares. Cut the squares diagonally into quarters to make 36 triangles. You will be using only 34 for side triangles.
- Cut 2, 6-inch squares. Cut the squares in half diagonally to make 4 corner triangles.

Quilt Center Assembly

Step 1 Referring to the quilt diagram, sew the pieced blocks, the alternate blocks, and the side triangles together in diagonal rows. Press the seam allowances in alternating directions by rows so the seams will fit snugly together with less bulk.

Step 2 Pin the rows at the block intersections; sew the rows together. Press the seam allowances in one direction.

Step 3 Sew the corner triangles to the quilt center; press.

Step 4 Trim away the excess fabric from the side and corner triangles, taking care to allow a 1/4-inch seam allowance beyond the corners of each block. Refer to **Trimming the Side and Corner Triangles** on page 212 for complete instructions.

Borders

Note: *The yardage given allows for the border strips to be cut on the crosswise grain. Diagonally piece the strips as needed, referring to* **Diagonal Piecing** *instructions on page 215. Read through* **Border** *instructions on page 214 for general instructions on adding borders.*

Cutting

From **WINE FLORAL:**
- Cut 9, 6-1/2 x 42-inch border strips
- Cut 1, 2-7/8 x 42-inch strip for sawtooth units

From **WINE PRINT:**
- Cut 1, 2-7/8 x 42-inch strip for sawtooth units

From **GOLD PLAID:**
- Cut 4, 6-1/2-inch corner squares

Assembling the Sawtooth Units

Step 1 With right sides together, layer the 2-7/8 x 42-inch **WINE PRINT** and **WINE FLORAL** strips together. Press together, but do not sew. Cut the layered strips into squares. Cut the layered squares in half diagonally to make 24 sets of triangles. Stitch 1/4-inch from the diagonal edge of each pair of triangles; press.

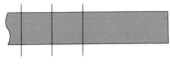

Crosscut 12, 2-7/8-inch squares

Make 24, 2-1/2-inch triangle-pieced squares

Step 2 Sew 3 of the triangle-pieced squares together for each sawtooth unit; press. <u>At this point each sawtooth unit should measure 2-1/2 x 6-1/2-inches.</u>

Make 4, sawtooth units

Make 4, sawtooth units

Attaching the Border

Step 1 To measure for the 6-1/2-inch wide **WINE FLORAL** top/bottom borders, refer to **Border** instructions on page 214. Subtract 4-inches from this measurement to allow for the sawtooth units at each end. Cut 2, 6-1/2-inch wide **WINE FLORAL** strips to this length.

Step 2 Referring to the quilt diagram, sew 2 sawtooth units to each end of the **WINE FLORAL** border strips; press. Sew the border strips to the top/bottom edges of the quilt; press.

Step 3 For the side borders, measure the quilt from top to bottom including the seam allowances but not the borders just added. Subtract 4-inches from this measurement to allow for the sawtooth units at each end. Cut 2, 6-1/2-inch wide **WINE FLORAL** strips to this length.

Step 4 Referring to the quilt diagram, sew 2 sawtooth units to each end of the **WINE FLORAL** strips; press. Sew the 6-1/2-inch **GOLD PLAID** corner squares to both ends of the border strips; press. Sew the border strips to the side edges of the quilt; press.

Putting It All Together

Cut the 7-7/8 yard length of backing fabric in thirds crosswise to make 3, 2-5/8 yard lengths. Refer to **Finishing the Quilt** on page 215 for complete instructions.

Binding

Cutting

From **RUST PLAID:**
- Cut enough 2-3/4-inch wide **bias** strips to make a 385-inch long strip.

Sew the binding to the quilt using a 3/8-inch seam allowance. This measurement will produce a 1/2-inch wide finished double binding. Refer to **Binding and Diagonal Piecing** instructions on page 215 for complete instructions.

Goldenrod Patch
Gold
88 x 96-inches

Color Book Garden

The ideal quilt for cottage decor or transitioning a little girl from the crib to her first "big" bed is one that can still be enjoyed even when she goes off to college. In this colorful quilt, checkerboard piecing, simple block construction, and stylized flowers and vines are gathered in a Color Book Garden.

Color Book Garden

78 x 94-inches

Fabrics & Supplies

1-1/2 yards **RED/BEIGE CHECK**
for blocks, border, and inner flower appliqués

1-1/4 yards **BLUE/GREEN/BEIGE PLAID**
for blocks and border

5/8 yard **LIGHT BLUE PRINT** for blocks

1-1/2 yards **RED PRINT**
for blocks and outer border

1/2 yard **GOLD PRINT**
for inner border and flower center appliqués

1-3/4 yards **BLUE PRINT** for checkerboard border,
nine-patch corner blocks, and flower appliqués

2-3/8 yards **BEIGE PRINT** for appliqué foundation,
checkerboard border, and nine-patch corner blocks

5/8 yard **GREEN/BEIGE CHECK**
for pieced border

1-1/4 yards **LIGHT GREEN PRINT**
for pieced border

1 yard **GREEN PRINT** for leaf and vine appliqués

7/8 yard **RED PRINT** for binding

5-3/4 yards backing fabric

quilt batting, at least 84 x 100-inches

paper-backed fusible web

lightweight cardboard for appliqués

#8 pearl cotton for decorative stitches: gold

Before beginning this project,
read through **Getting Started** on page 210.

Pieced Blocks

Makes 17 blocks

Cutting

From **RED/BEIGE CHECK:**
• Cut 2, 2-1/2 x 42-inch strips. From the strips cut:
  17, 2-1/2-inch squares

From **BLUE/GREEN/BEIGE PLAID:**
• Cut 7, 1-1/2 x 42-inch strips

From **LIGHT BLUE PRINT:**
• Cut 11, 1-1/2 x 42-inch strips

From **RED PRINT:**
• Cut 15, 1-1/2 x 42-inch strips

Piecing

Step 1   Sew a 1-1/2-inch wide
BLUE/GREEN/BEIGE PLAID strip
to the top/bottom edges of a 2-1/2-inch
RED/BEIGE CHECK square. Press the seam
allowance toward the strips; trim the strips
even with the edges of the square.

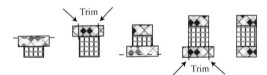

Step 2   Sew a 1-1/2-inch wide
BLUE/GREEN/BEIGE PLAID strip to
both side edges of the unit; press and trim.

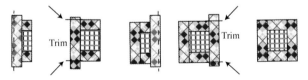

Step 3   Continue by adding the 1-1/2-inch wide
LIGHT BLUE strips to the top/bottom edges of
the unit, and to the side edges of the unit; press and
trim. Sew the 1-1/2-inch wide **RED** strips to the
top/bottom edges of the unit, and to the side edges of
the unit; press and trim. <u>At this point each pieced
block should measure 8-1/2-inches square.</u>

Make 17

Appliqué the Blocks and Borders

Makes 18 blocks

Cutting

From **BEIGE PRINT**:
- Cut 5, 8-1/2 x 42-inch strips. From the strips cut:
  18, 8-1/2-inch appliqué foundation squares

From **LIGHT GREEN PRINT**:
- Cut 5, 6-1/2 x 42-inch strips. From the strips cut
  and piece:
  2, 6-1/2 x 50-1/2-inch rectangles for border
  appliqué foundations
  2, 6-1/2 x 34-1/2-inch rectangles for border
  appliqué foundations

From **GREEN/BEIGE CHECK**:
- Cut 3, 6-1/2 x 42-inch strips. From the strips cut:
  8, 6-1/2 x 10-1/2-inch rectangles for
  pieced border

From **GREEN PRINT**:
- Cut enough 1-3/4-inch wide **bias** strips to total
  220-inches. Diagonally piece the strips
  as needed.
  Cut 2 vines 46-inches long for the
  top/bottom borders
  Cut 2 vines 62-inches long for the
  side borders

Fusible Web Appliqué Method

Prepare the Flowers and Leaves

Step 1 Position the fusible web (paper side up)
over the flower A, flower B, leaf D, and leaf E
shapes. With a pencil, trace the shapes the
number of times as indicated on each pattern,
leaving a small margin between each shape.
Cut the shapes apart.

Note: *When you fuse a large shape like the flower, fuse just
the outer edges of the shape so that it will not look stiff when
finished. To do this, draw a line about 3/8-inch inside the
flower and cut away the fusible web on this line.*

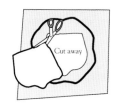

Step 2 Following the manufacturer's instructions,
fuse the shapes to the wrong side of the fabrics
chosen for the appliqués. Let the fabric cool and
cut along the traced line of each shape. Peel away
the paper backing from the fusible web. Set the
leaves aside.

Cardboard Appliqué Method

Prepare the Flower Centers

Step 1 Make a cardboard template using the
flower center C pattern.

Step 2 Position the template on the wrong side of
the fabric chosen for the flower center and trace
around the template 42 times leaving a 3/4-inch
margin around each shape. Remove the template
and cut a scant 1/4-inch beyond the drawn lines.

Step 3 To create smooth, round circles, run a line
of basting stitches around the circle, placing the
stitches halfway between the drawn line and the cut
edge of the circle. After basting, keep the needle
and thread attached for the next step.

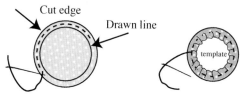

Make 42 flower centers

Step 4 Place the cardboard template on the
wrong side of the fabric circle and gently pull
on the basting stitches, gathering the fabric over
the template. When the thread is tight, space
the gathers evenly and make a knot to secure
the thread. Clip the thread, press the circle,
and remove the cardboard template. Make 42
flower centers.

Step 5 Pin the flower centers to the **BLUE** B
flowers and the **RED/BEIGE CHECK** B flowers,
and hand appliqué in place using matching thread.

Blanket stitch around the flower centers with gold pearl cotton.

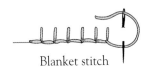
Blanket stitch

Step 6   Pin 18 of the **RED/BEIGE CHECK** flower units to the **BLUE** A flowers, fuse in place and machine appliqué using a zigzag stitch with matching thread.

Appliqué the Blocks

Referring to the block diagram, position the D leaves and the A/B/C flower units on the 8-1/2-inch **BEIGE** appliqué foundation squares. Layer the shapes as diagramed and machine appliqué in place using a zigzag stitch with matching thread. Set the appliquéd blocks aside.

Prepare the Vines

Fold each 1-3/4-inch wide **GREEN** bias strip in half lengthwise with wrong sides together; press. To keep the raw edges aligned, stitch a scant 1/4-inch away from the edges. Fold each strip in half again so the raw edges are hidden by the first folded edge; press.

Appliqué the Borders

Step 1   Referring to the quilt diagram, position the 46-inch long vines on the 6-1/2 x 34-1/2-inch **LIGHT GREEN** rectangles; pin in place. Position the E leaves and the B/C flower units on the **LIGHT GREEN** border rectangles; pin in place. Hand appliqué the vines in place with matching thread. Machine appliqué the flowers and leaves in place with a zigzag stitch and matching thread.

Step 2   Referring to the quilt diagram, position the 62-inch long vines on the 6-1/2 x 50-1/2-inch **LIGHT GREEN** rectangles; pin in place. Position the E leaves and the B/C flower units on the **LIGHT GREEN** border rectangles; pin in place. Hand appliqué the vines in place with matching thread. Machine appliqué the flowers and leaves in place with a zigzag stitch and matching thread.

Step 3   Sew a 6-1/2 x 10-1/2-inch **GREEN/BEIGE CHECK** rectangle to both ends of each of the appliquéd border rectangles. The top/bottom appliquéd border strips should measure 6-1/2 x 54-1/2-inches. The side appliquéd border strips should measure 6-1/2 x 70-1/2-inches. Set the border strips aside.

Quilt Center

Assembling the Quilt Center

Step 1   Referring to the quilt diagram for block placement, sew together the pieced blocks and appliquéd blocks in 7 horizontal rows of 5 blocks each.

Step 2   Press the seam allowances in alternating directions by rows so the seams will fit snugly together with less bulk.

Step 3   Pin the rows together at the block intersections; stitch. Press the seam allowances in one direction. At this point the quilt center should measure 40-1/2 x 56-1/2-inches.

Borders

Note: *The yardage given allows for the border strips to be cut on the crosswise grain. Diagonally piece the strips as needed, referring to **Diagonal Piecing** instructions on page 215 for complete instructions. Read through **Border** instructions on page 214 for general instructions on adding borders.*

Cutting

From **GOLD PRINT:**
• Cut 5, 1-1/2 x 42-inch inner border strips

From **BLUE PRINT:**
• Cut 12, 2-1/2 x 42-inch strips for checkerboard border and nine-patch corner squares

From **BEIGE PRINT:**
• Cut 12, 2-1/2 x 42-inch strips for checkerboard border and nine-patch corner squares

From **RED/BEIGE CHECK:**
• Cut 8, 2-1/2 x 42-inch border strips

From **BLUE/GREEN/BEIGE PLAID:**
• Cut 8, 2-1/2 x 42-inch border strips

From **RED PRINT:**
- Cut 9, 2-1/2 x 42-inch outer border strips

Assembling and Attaching the Borders

Step 1   Attach the 1-1/2-inch wide **GOLD** inner border strips.

Step 2   Aligning long edges, sew a 2-1/2 x 42-inch **BLUE** strip to both side edges of a 2-1/2 x 42-inch **BEIGE** strip. Press the seam allowances toward the **BLUE** strips. Make 4 strip sets. Cut the strip sets into segments.

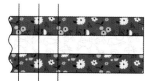

Crosscut 64, 2-1/2-inch wide segments

Step 3   Aligning long edges, sew a 2-1/2 x 42-inch **BEIGE** strip to both sides of a 2-1/2 x 42-inch **BLUE** strip. Press the seam allowances toward the **BLUE** strip. Make 4 strip sets. Cut the strips sets into segments.

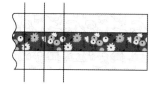

Crosscut 60, 2-1/2-inch wide segments

Step 4   To make a nine-patch block, sew a Step 2 segment to the top/ bottom edges of a Step 3 segment; press. Make 4 blocks. <u>At this point each nine-patch block should measure 6-1/2-inches square.</u>

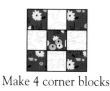

Make 4 corner blocks

Step 5   To make the top/bottom checkerboard borders, sew together 10 of the Step 2 segments and 11 of the Step 3 segments; press. Sew the borders to the quilt; press.

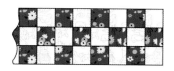

Step 6   For the side borders, sew together 18 of the Step 2 segments and 17 of the Step 3 segments; press. Sew the borders to the quilt; press. <u>At this point the quilt center should measure 54-1/2 x 70-1/2-inches.</u>

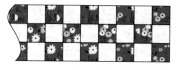

Step 7   Attach the 6-1/2 x 54-1/2-inch top/bottom appliquéd borders to the quilt; press. For the side borders, sew a nine-patch corner block to both ends of the 6-1/2 x 70-1/2-inch side appliquéd borders; press. Sew the borders to the quilt; press.

Step 8   Attach the 2-1/2-inch wide **RED/BEIGE CHECK** border strips.

Step 9   Attach the 2-1/2-inch wide **BLUE/GREEN/BEIGE PLAID** border strips.

Step 10   Attach the 2-1/2-inch wide **RED** outer border strips.

Putting It All Together

Cut the 5-3/4 yard length of backing fabric in half crosswise to make 2, 2-7/8 yard lengths. Refer to **Finishing the Quilt** on page 215 for complete instructions.

Binding

Cutting

From **RED PRINT:**
- Cut 9, 2-3/4 x 42-inch wide strips

Sew the binding to the quilt using a 3/8-inch seam allowance. This measurement will produce a 1/2-inch wide finished double binding. Refer to **Binding and Diagonal Piecing** on page 215 for complete instructions.

Color Book Garden Templates

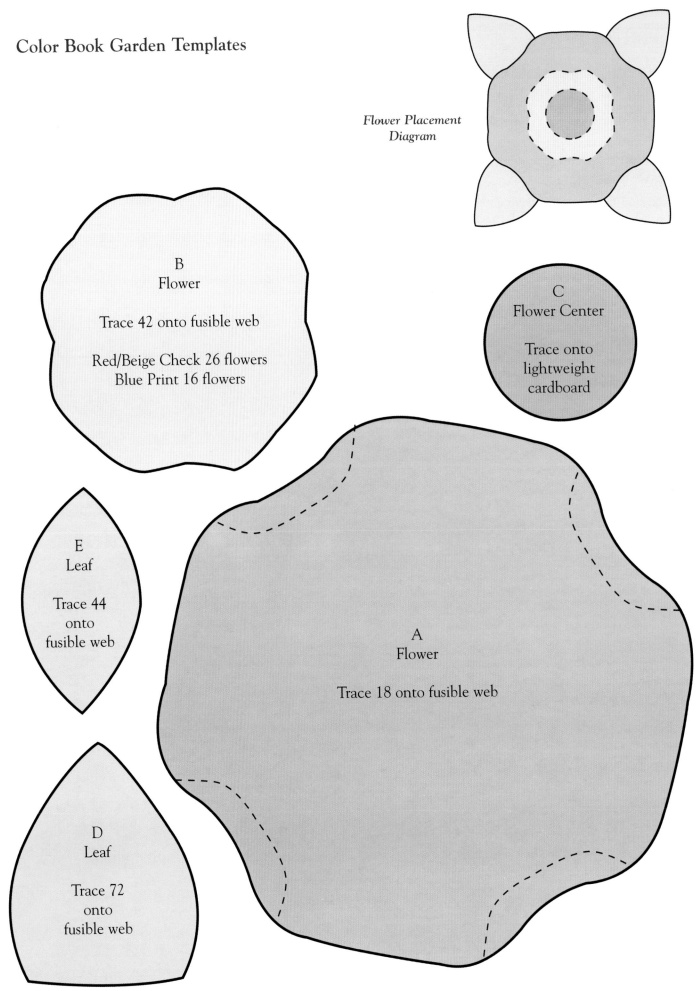

Flower Placement Diagram

B
Flower

Trace 42 onto fusible web

Red/Beige Check 26 flowers
Blue Print 16 flowers

C
Flower Center

Trace onto
lightweight
cardboard

E
Leaf

Trace 44
onto
fusible web

A
Flower

Trace 18 onto fusible web

D
Leaf

Trace 72
onto
fusible web

Color Book Garden

78 x 94-inches

Holly Goose Chase

Transform the bedroom into a holiday
extravaganza with a touch of appliquéd
holly leaves and berries accented with
easy embroidery that elevates this simple
quilt into a real show-stopper. Holly
Goose Chase is sure to be a true
heirloom for your quilt collection.

Holly Goose Chase

80 x 98-inches

Fabrics & Supplies

1-3/8 yards **RED PRINT**
for blocks and berry appliqués

2-1/2 yards **BEIGE PRINT #1** for blocks

1-1/4 yards **BEIGE PRINT #2** for blocks

1-1/4 yards **BEIGE PRINT #3** for blocks

1-3/8 yards **GREEN PRINT #1** for lattice strips

3/4 yard **CHESTNUT PRINT**
for center squares, lattice posts, and corner squares

3/8 yard *each* of **GREEN PRINT #2** and
GREEN PRINT #3 for leaf appliqués

2 yards **RED FLORAL** for outer border

1 yard **GREEN PRINT #1** for binding

7 yards backing fabric

quilt batting, at least 86 x 104-inches

freezer paper for appliqués and embroidery template

lightweight cardboard for appliqués

#8 pearl cotton or embroidery floss
for decorative stitches: gold

Before beginning this project,
read through **Getting Started** on page 210.

Pieced Blocks

Makes 12 blocks

Cutting

From **RED PRINT:**
- Cut 9, 4-1/2 x 42-inch strips. From the strips cut:
  144, 2-1/2 x 4-1/2-inch rectangles

From **BEIGE PRINT #1:**
- Cut 18, 2-1/2 x 42-inch strips. From the strips cut:
  288, 2-1/2-inch squares
- Cut 8 more 2-1/2 x 42-inch strips for strip sets

From *each* of **BEIGE PRINT #2** and **#3:**
- Cut 8, 2-1/2 x 42-inch strips for strip sets

From **CHESTNUT PRINT:**
- Cut 2, 4-1/2 x 42-inch strips. From the strips cut:
  12, 4-1/2-inch center squares

Piecing

Step 1   With right sides together, position a
2-1/2-inch **BEIGE #1** square on the corner of a
2-1/2 x 4-1/2-inch **RED** rectangle. Draw a diagonal
line on the square and stitch on the line. Trim the
seam allowance to 1/4-inch; press. Repeat this process
at the opposite corner of the rectangle.

Make 144

Step 2   Sew 3 of the Step 1 units together; press.
At this point each flying geese unit should measure
4-1/2 x 6-1/2-inches.

Make 48

Step 3   Sew a flying geese unit to both side
edges of a 4-1/2-inch **CHESTNUT** square; press.
At this point each section should measure
4-1/2 x 16-1/2-inches.

Make 12

Step 4   Aligning long edges, sew together the
2-1/2 x 42-inch **BEIGE PRINT #1, #2,** and **#3**
strips. Press the seam allowances in one direction.

Make a total of 8 strip sets, sewing the strips together in a random fashion. Cut the strip sets into segments.

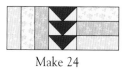

Crosscut 48, 6-1/2-inch wide segments

Step 5 Referring to the diagram for placement, sew Step 4 segments to both side edges of the remaining Step 2 flying geese units. Press the seam allowances toward the Step 4 segments. At this point each section should measure 6-1/2 x 16-1/2-inches.

Make 24

Step 6 Sew Step 5 sections to both side edges of a Step 3 section to complete the block; press. At this point each pieced block should measure 16-1/2-inches square.

Make 24

Quilt Center

Cutting

From GREEN PRINT #1:
- Cut 16, 2-1/2 x 42-inch strips.
    From the strips cut:
    31, 2-1/2 x 16-1/2-inch lattice segments

From CHESTNUT PRINT:
- Cut 2, 2-1/2 x 42-inch strips. From the strips cut:
    20, 2-1/2-inch lattice post squares

Quilt Center Assembly

Step 1 Sew together 3 pieced blocks and 4 of the 2-1/2 x 16-1/2-inch **GREEN #1** lattice segments. Press the seam allowances toward the **GREEN**

lattice segments. At this point each block row should measure 16-1/2 x 56-1/2-inches.

Make 4 block rows

Step 2 Sew together 3 of the 2-1/2 x 16-1/2-inch **GREEN #1** lattice segments and 4 of the 2-1/2-inch **CHESTNUT** lattice post squares. Press the seam allowances toward the **GREEN** lattice segments. At this point each lattice strip should measure 2-1/2 x 56-1/2-inches.

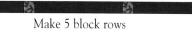

Make 5 block rows

Step 3 Referring to the quilt diagram for placement, pin the block rows and lattice strips together at the block intersections. Sew the strips together; press the seam allowances in one direction. At this point the quilt center should measure 56-1/2 x 74-1/2-inches.

Borders

Note: *The yardage given allows for the border strips to be cut on the crosswise grain. Diagonally piece the strips as needed, referring to* **Diagonal Piecing** *instructions on page 215. Read through* **Border** *instructions on page 214 for general instructions on adding borders.*

Cutting

From *each* of BEIGE PRINT #1, #2, and #3:
- Cut 7, 2-1/2 x 42-inch strips for the strip sets

From the remaining BEIGE PRINTS:
- Cut a total of 4, 2-1/2 x 6-1/2-inch rectangles to be added to the pieced borders

From CHESTNUT PRINT:
- Cut 1, 6-1/2 x 42-inch strip. From this strip cut:
    4, 6-1/2-inch corner squares

From RED FLORAL:
- Cut 10, 6-1/2 x 42-inch outer border strips

Assembling and Attaching the Borders

Step 1 Aligning long edges, sew together one of each of the 2-1/2 x 42-inch **BEIGE PRINT #1, #2,** and **#3** strips. Press the seam allowances in one direction. Make a total of 8 strip sets, sewing the strips together in a random fashion. Cut the strip sets into segments.

Crosscut 42, 6-1/2-inch wide segments

Step 2 Referring to the quilt diagram for placement, sew together 9 of the Step 1 segments. Sew a 2-1/2 x 6-1/2-inch **BEIGE** rectangle to one end of the strip to complete the top pieced border; press. At this point the top pieced border should measure 6-1/2 x 56-1/2-inches. Sew the border strip to the top edge of the quilt; press. Repeat this process for the bottom border.

Step 3 Referring to the quilt diagram for placement, sew together 12 of the Step 1 segments. Sew 1 of the 2-1/2 x 6-1/2-inch **BEIGE** rectangles to 1 end of the strip to complete a side pieced border; press. At this point the pieced border should measure 6-1/2 x 74-1/2-inches. Sew 6-1/2-inch **CHESTNUT** corner squares to both ends of the side pieced border; press. Sew the border strip to the side edge of the quilt; press. Repeat this process for the remaining side border.

Step 4 Attach the 6-1/2-inch wide **RED FLORAL** outer border strips.

Appliqué

The appliqué shapes are on page 202. The embroidery design template is on page 202. The decorative stitch diagram is on page 201.

Embroider the Vines and Tendrils

Step 1 To mark the borders for embroidery, cut a 6 x 20-inch sheet of freezer paper. Trace the vine and tendril design onto the paper side of the freezer paper. Using a small sharp scissors,

carefully cut away a 1/8-inch space along the vine and tendrils as if making a quilt stencil.

Step 2 Position the freezer paper on the pieced border; iron in place. Lightly trace the vine and tendrils on the border; remove the freezer paper. Mark the remaining borders in this manner. The freezer paper template may be reused.

Step 3 With gold pearl cotton or 3 strands of embroidery floss, stitch the vine and tendrils with the outline/stem stitch.

Freezer Paper Appliqué Method

Appliqué the Holly Leaves

Step 1 To prepare the holly leaf appliqués, lay the freezer paper, paper side up, over the leaf shape. With a pencil, trace leaf Pattern A 28 times and leaf Pattern A reversed 42 times.

Step 2 With a dry iron on the wool setting, press the coated side of the freezer paper leaves onto the wrong side of the **GREEN PRINT #2** and **#3** fabrics, allowing 1/2-inch between each shape.

Step 3 Cut out each leaf a scant 1/4-inch beyond the freezer paper edge. Clip curved edges close to the paper if needed. Finger press the fabric seam allowance around the edge of the freezer paper.

Step 4 Referring to the quilt diagram for placement, position the leaves on the borders; hand baste in place. Using matching thread, appliqué the leaves in place.

Note: *When there is about 1-inch left to appliqué, remove the freezer paper. Slide your needle into this opening to loosen the freezer paper from the fabric. Gently pull the freezer paper out. Finish stitching the appliqué in place.*

Step 5 Mark the veins on the leaves. Outline/stem stitch the veins with gold pearl cotton or 3 strands of embroidery floss.

Cardboard Appliqué Method

Appliqué the Berries

Step 1 Make several lightweight cardboard templates using berry Pattern B on page 202.

Step 2 Position a berry template on the wrong side of the **RED** fabric; trace around the template. Trace 98 berries allowing a 3/4-inch space between each shape. Remove the template and cut a scant 1/4-inch beyond the drawn line of each shape.

Step 3 To create smooth round circles, run a line of small basting stitches around the circle, placing the stitches halfway between the drawn line and the cut edge. After basting the circle, keep the needle and thread attached for Step 4.

Step 4 Place the cardboard template on the wrong side of the fabric circle and tug on the basting stitches, gathering the fabric over the template. When the thread is tight, space the gathers evenly; knot the thread to secure it. Clip the thread, press the circle on both sides, and remove the template.

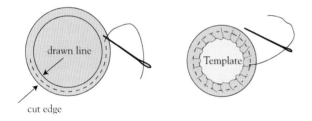

Step 5 Referring to the quilt diagram for placement, position the berries on the borders; hand baste in place. Using matching thread, appliqué the berries in place.

Putting It All Together

Cut the 7 yard length of backing fabric in thirds crosswise to make 3, 2-1/3 yard lengths. Refer to **Finishing the Quilt** on page 215 for complete instructions.

Binding

Cutting

From **GREEN PRINT #1:**
• Cut 10, 2-3/4 x 42-inch strips

Sew the binding to the quilt using a 3/8-inch seam allowance. This measurement will produce a 1/2-inch wide finished double binding. Refer to **Binding** and **Diagonal Piecing** on page 215 for complete instructions.

Decorative Stitch
Outline/Stem Stitch

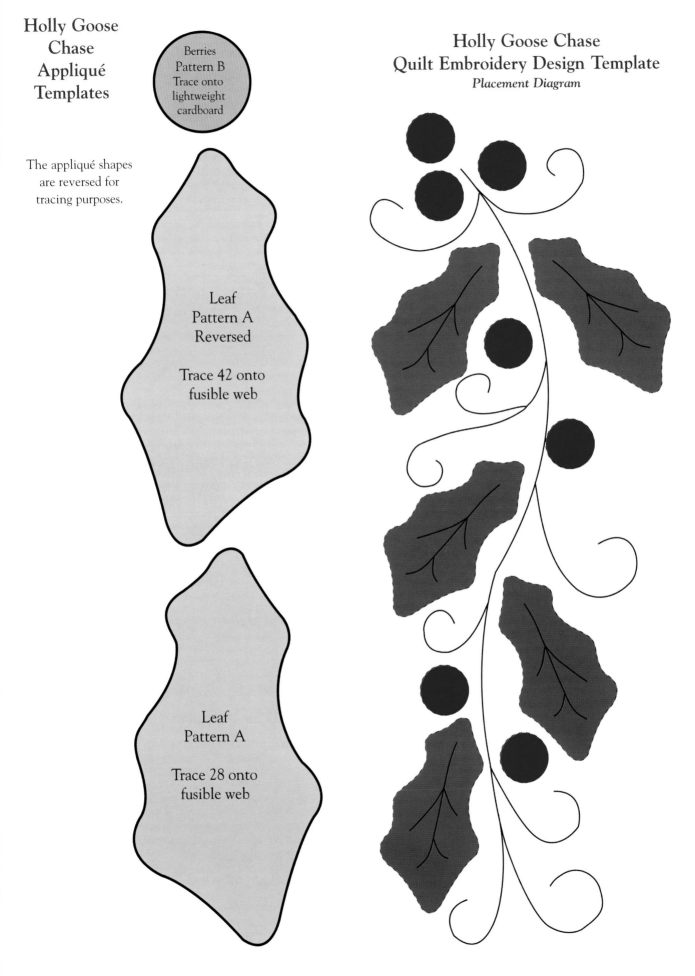

Holly Goose Chase Appliqué Templates

Berries
Pattern B
Trace onto lightweight cardboard

The appliqué shapes are reversed for tracing purposes.

Leaf
Pattern A
Reversed

Trace 42 onto fusible web

Leaf
Pattern A

Trace 28 onto fusible web

Holly Goose Chase Quilt Embroidery Design Template
Placement Diagram

Holly Goose Chase

80 x 98-inches

Sweet Retreat
Comforter

The twin-sized Sweet Retreat comforter is
just right for tea for two or breakfast in
bed. A soft comfort for casual weekends in
a cottage or cabin setting, the top works up
quickly with a beige floral used for the
large center panel and outer border.

Sweet Retreat
Comforter

88 x 100-inches

5-7/8 yards **LARGE BEIGE FLORAL**
for center panel and outer border

1-1/8 yards **GREEN PRINT** for inner border

1-5/8 yards **PINK PRINT** for flying geese

1-5/8 yards **BEIGE PRINT** for flying geese

1/4 yard **GREEN FLORAL** for corner squares

1-1/8 yards **GREEN PLAID**
for binding (cut on the bias)

7-7/8 yards backing fabric

quilt batting, at least 94 x 106-inches

Before beginning this project,
read through **Getting Started** on page 210.

Comforter Top

Cutting

From **GREEN PRINT**:
• Cut 7, 4-1/2 x 42-inch inner border strips

From **PINK PRINT**:
• Cut 8, 6-1/2 x 42-inch strips. From the strips cut:
    22, 6-1/2 x 12-1/2-inch rectangles

From **BEIGE PRINT**:
• Cut 8, 6-1/2 x 42-inch strips. From the strips cut:
    44, 6-1/2-inch squares

From **GREEN FLORAL**:
• Cut 4, 6-1/2-inch corner squares

From **LARGE BEIGE FLORAL**:
• Cut 1, 3 yard length for center panel
• Cut 11, 8-1/2 x 42-inch outer border strips

Piecing

Note: *The yardage given allows for the border strips to be cut on the crosswise grain. Diagonally piece the strips as needed, referring to* **Diagonal Piecing** *instructions on page 215. Read through* **Border** *instructions on page 214 for general instructions on adding borders.*

Step 1 Cut the 3 yard length of **LARGE BEIGE FLORAL** in half crosswise to make 2, 1-1/2 yard lengths. Remove the selvages from the fabric. Sew the long edges together; press. Trim the center panel to 52-1/2 x 64-1/2-inches.

Step 2 Attach the 4-1/2-inch wide **GREEN PRINT** inner border strips.

Step 3 With right sides together, position a 6-1/2-inch **BEIGE** square on the corner of a 6-1/2 x 12-1/2-inch **PINK** rectangle. Draw a diagonal line on the square and stitch on the line. Trim the seam allowance to 1/4-inch; press. Repeat this process at the opposite corner of the rectangle.

Make 22 flying geese units

Step 4 Sew 5 flying geese units together for the top/bottom borders; press. Sew the border strips to the top/bottom edges of the quilt; press.

Step 5   Sew 6 flying geese units together for each side border; press. Sew 6-1/2-inch **GREEN FLORAL** corner squares to both ends of each flying geese border strip; press. Sew a border strip to each side edge of the quilt; press.

Step 6   Attach the 8-1/2-inch wide **LARGE BEIGE FLORAL** outer border strips.

Putting It All Together

Cut the 7-7/8 yard length of backing fabric in thirds crosswise to make 3, 2-5/8 yard lengths. Refer to **Finishing the Quilt** on page 215 for complete instructions.

Binding

Cutting

From **GREEN PLAID:**
• Cut enough 2-3/4-inch wide **bias** strips to make a 400-inch long strip.

Sew the binding to the quilt using a 3/8-inch seam allowance. This measurement will produce a 1/2-inch wide finished double binding. Refer to **Binding and Diagonal Piecing** on page 215 for complete instructions.

Sweet Retreat
Comforter
88 x 100-inches

RESOURCES

Quilting is an art, not a science. However, to make the best use of your time and materials, it is important to be familiar with the tried and true method that Lynette Jensen has developed for easy cutting, piecing, appliqué, and quilting.

Begin by reading the General Instructions thoroughly. When you've finished, choose a quilt that suits your style and need (for reference, a small photo of each quilt accompanies its listing in the Project Index.)

Save the Quilting Guides for last. When you've completed your quilting project, you'll have a better idea of what you'll want to add for the finishing touches. But most of all, throughout the creative and soul-satisfying process of quilting—enjoy!

Getting Started

Yardage is based on 42-inch wide fabric. If your fabric is wider or narrower, it will affect the amount of necessary strips you need to cut in some patterns, and of course, it will affect the amount of fabric you have left over. Generally, Thimbleberries® patterns allow for a little extra fabric so you can confidently cut your pattern pieces with ease.

A rotary cutter, mat, and wide clear plastic ruler with 1/8-inch markings are needed tools in attaining accuracy. A beginner needs good tools just as an experienced quilt-maker needs good equipment. A 24 x 36-inch mat board is a good size to own. It will easily accommodate the average quilt fabrics and will aid in accurate cutting. The plastic ruler you purchase should be at least 6 x 24 inches and easy to read. Do not purchase a smaller ruler to save money. The large size will be invaluable to your quilt-making success.

It is often recommended to prewash and press fabrics to test for color fastness and possible shrinkage. If you choose to prewash, wash in cool water and dry in a cool to moderate dryer. Industry standards actually suggest that line drying is best. Shrinkage is generally very minimal and usually is not a concern. A good way to test your fabric for both shrinkage and color fastness is to cut a 3-inch square of fabric. Soak the fabric in a white bowl filled with water. Squeeze the water out of the fabric and press it dry on a piece of muslin. If the fabric is going to release color, it will do so either in the water or when it is pressed dry. Remeasure the 3-inch fabric square to see if it has changed size considerably (more than

1/4- inch). If it has, wash, dry, and press the entire yardage. This little test could save you hours in prewashing and pressing.

Read instructions thoroughly before beginning a project. Each step will make more sense to you when you have a general overview of the whole process. Take one step at a time and follow the illustrations. They will often make more sense to you than the words. Take "baby steps" so you don't get overwhelmed by the entire process.

When working with flannel and other loosely woven fabrics, always prewash and dry. These fabrics almost always shrink more.

For piecing, place right sides of the fabric pieces together and use 1/4-inch seam allowances throughout the entire quilt unless otherwise specifically stated in the directions. An accurate seam allowance is the most important part of the quilt-making process after accurately cutting. All the directions are based on accurate 1/4-inch seam allowances. It is very important to check your sewing machine to see what position your fabric should be to get accurate seams. To test, use a piece of 1/4-inch graph paper, stitch along the quarter inch line as if the paper were fabric. Make note of where the edge of the paper lines up with your presser foot or where it lines up on the throat of the plate of your machine. Many quilters place a piece of masking tape on the throat plate to help guide the edge of the fabric. Now test your seam allowance on fabric. Cut 2, 2-1/2-inch squares, place right sides together and stitch along one edge. Press seam allowances in one direction and measure. At this point the unit should measure 2-1/2 x 4-1/2-inches. If it does not, adjust your stitching guidelines and test again. Seam allowances are included in the cutting sizes given in this book.

Pressing is the third most important step in quilt-making. As a general rule, you should never cross a stitched seam with another seam unless it has been pressed. Therefore, every time you stitch a seam, it needs to be pressed before adding another piece. Often, it will feel like you press as much as you sew, and often that is true. It is very important that you press and not iron the seams. Pressing is a firm, up-and-down motion that will flatten the seams but not distort the piecing. Ironing is a back-and-forth motion and will stretch and distort the small pieces. Most quilters use steam to help the pressing process. The moisture does help and will not distort the shapes as long as the pressing motion is used.

An old-fashioned rule is to press seam allowances in one direction, toward the darker fabric. Often, background fabrics are light in color and pressing toward the darker fabric prevents the seam allowances from showing through to the right side. Pressing seam allowances in one direction is thought to create a stronger seam. Also, for ease in hand-quilting, the quilting lines should fall on the side of the seam which is opposite the seam allowance. As you piece quilts, you will find these "rules" to be helpful but not neccesarily always appropriate. Sometimes seams need to be pressed in the opposite direction so the seams of different units will fit together more easily, which quilters refer to as seams "nesting" together. When sewing together two units with opposing seam allowances, use the tip of your seam ripper to gently guide the units under your presser foot. Sometimes it is necessary to re-press the seams to make the units fit together nicely. Always try to achieve the least bulk in one spot and accept that no matter which way you press, it may be a little tricky and it could be a little bulky.

Pressing Direction

Pressing Direction

Squaring Up Blocks

To square up your blocks, first check the seam allowances. This is usually where the problem is, and it is always best to alter within the block rather than trim the outer edges. Next, make sure you have pressed accurately. Sometimes a block can become distorted by ironing instead of pressing.

To trim up block edges, use one of many clear plastic squares available on the market. Determine the center of the block; mark with a pin. Lay the square over the block and align as many perpendicular and horizontal lines as you can to the seams in your block. This will indicate where the block is off.

Do not trim all off on one side; this usually results in real distortion of the pieces in the block and the block design. Take a little off all sides until the block is square. When assembling many blocks, it is necessary to make sure *all* are the same size.

Tools and Equipment

Making beautiful quilts does not require a large number of specialized tools or expensive equipment. My list of favorites is short and sweet and includes the things I use over and over again because they are always accurate and dependable.

I find a long acrylic ruler indispensable for accurate rotary cutting. The ones I like most are an Omnigrid 6 x 24-inch grid acrylic ruler for cutting long strips and squaring up fabrics and quilt tops and a Masterpiece 45, 8 x 24-inch ruler for cutting 6- to 8-inch wide borders. I sometimes tape together two 6 x 24-inch acrylic rulers for cutting borders up to 12 inches wide.

A 15-inch Omnigrid square acrylic ruler is great for squaring up individual blocks and corners of a quilt top, for cutting strips up to 15 inches wide or long, and for trimming side and corner triangles.

I think the markings on my 23 x 35-inch Olfa rotary cutting mat stay visible longer than on other mats, and the lines are fine and accurate.

The largest size Olfa rotary cutter cuts through many layers of fabric easily, and it isn't cumbersome to use. The 2-1/2-inch blade slices through three layers of backing, batting, and a quilt top like butter.

An 8-inch pair of Gingher shears is great for cutting out appliqué templates and cutting fabric from a bolt or fabric scraps.

I keep a pair of 5-1/2-inch Gingher scissors by my sewing machine so it is handy for both machine work and handwork. This size is versatile and sharp enough to make large and small cuts equally well.

My Grabbit magnetic pin cushion has a surface that is large enough to hold lots of straight pins and a strong magnet that keeps them securely in place.

Silk pins are long and thin, which means they won't leave large holes in your fabric. I like them because they increase accuracy in pinning pieces or blocks together and it is easy to press over silk pins as well.

For pressing individual pieces, blocks, and quilt tops, I use an 18 x 48-inch sheet of plywood covered with several layers of cotton fiberfill and topped with a layer of muslin stapled to the back. The 48-inch length allows me to press an entire width of fabric at one time without the need to reposition it, and the square ends are better than tapered ends on an ironing board for pressing finished quilt tops.

Rotary Cutting

SAFETY FIRST! The blades of a rotary cutter are very sharp and need to be for accurate cutting. Look at a variety of cutters to find one that feels good in your hand. All quality cutters have a safety mechanism to "close" the cutting blade when not in use. After each cut and before laying the rotary cutter down, close the blade. Soon this will become second nature to you and will prevent dangerous accidents. Always keep cutters out of the sight of children. Rotary cutters are very tempting to fiddle with when they are lying around. When your blade is dull or nicked, change it. Damaged blades do not cut accurately and require extra effort that can also result in slipping and injury. Also, always cut away from yourself for safety.

Fold the fabric in half lengthwise matching the selvage edges.

"Square off" the ends of your fabric before measuring and cutting pieces. This means that the cut edge of the fabric must be exactly perpendicular to the folded edge which creates a 90° angle. Align the folded and selvage edges of the fabric with the lines on the

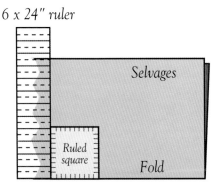

6 x 24" ruler

cutting board, and place a ruled square on the fold. Place a 6 x 24-inch ruler against the side of the square to get a 90° angle. Hold the ruler in place, remove the square, and cut along the edge of the ruler. If you are left-handed, work from the other end of the fabric. Use the lines on your cutting board to help line up fabric, but not to measure and cut strips. Use a ruler for accurate cutting, always checking to make sure your fabric is lined up with horizontal and vertical lines on the ruler.

Cutting Strips

When cutting strips or rectangles, cut on the crosswise grain. Strips can then be cut into squares or smaller rectangles.

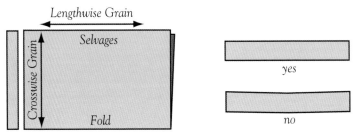

If your strips are not straight after cutting a few of them, refold the fabric, align the folded and selvage edges with the lines on the cutting board, and "square off" the edge again by trimming to straighten, and begin cutting.

Trimming Side and Corner Triangles

In projects with side and corner triangles, the instructions have you cut side and corner triangles larger than needed. This will allow you to square up the quilt and eliminates the frustration of ending up with precut side and corner triangles that don't match the size of your pieced blocks.

To cut triangles, first cut squares. The project directions will tell you what size to make the squares and whether to cut them in half to make two triangles

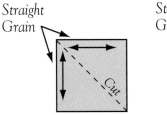

Corner Triangles

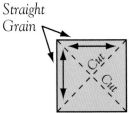

Side Triangles

or to cut them in quarters to make four triangles, as shown in the diagrams. This cutting method will give you side triangles that have the straight grain on the outside edges of the quilt. This is a very important part of quilt-making that will help stabilize your quilt center.

Helpful Hints for Sewing with Flannel

Always prewash and machine dry flannel. This will prevent severe shrinkage after the quilt is made. Some flannels shrink more than others. For this reason, we have allowed approximately 1/4 yard extra for each fabric under the fabric requirements. Treat the more heavily napped side of solid flannels as the right side of the fabric.

Because flannel stretches more than other cotton calicos and because the nap makes them thicker, the quilt design should be simple. Let the fabric and color make the design statement.

Consider combining regular cotton calicos with flannels. The different textures complement each other nicely.

Use a 10 to 12 stitches per inch setting on your machine. A 1/4-inch seam allowance is also recommended for flannel piecing.

When sewing triangle-pieced squares together, take extra care not to stretch the diagonal seam. Trim off the points from the seam allowances to eliminate bulk.

Press gently to prevent stretching pieces out of shape.

Check block measurements as you progress. "Square up" the blocks as needed. Flannel will shift and it is easy to end up with blocks that are misshapen. If you trim and measure as you go, you are more likely to have accurate blocks. If you notice a piece of flannel is stretching more than the others, place it on the bottom when stitching on the machine. The natural action of the feed dogs will help prevent it from stretching.

Before stitching pieces, strips, or borders together, pin often to prevent fabric from stretching and moving. When stitching longer pieces together, divide the pieces into quarters and pin. Divide into even smaller sections to get more control.

Use a lightweight batting to prevent the quilt from becoming too heavy.

Cutting Triangles from Squares

Cutting accurate triangles can be intimidating for beginners, but a clear plastic ruler, rotary cutter, and cutting mat are all that are needed to make perfect triangles. The cutting instructions often direct you to cut strips, then squares, and then triangles.

Sewing Layered Strips Together

When you are instructed to layer strips, right sides together, and sew, you need to take some precautions. Gently lay a strip on top of another, carefully lining up the raw edges. Pressing the strips together will hold them together nicely, and a few pins here and there will also help. Be careful not to stretch the strips as you sew them together.

Rod Casing or Sleeve to Hang Quilts

To hang wall quilts, attach a casing that is made of the same fabric as the quilt back. Attach this casing at the top of the quilt, just below the binding. Often, it is helpful to attach a second casing at the bottom of the quilt so you can insert a dowel into it which will help weight the quilt and make it hang free of ripples.

To make a rod casing or "sleeve," cut enough strips of fabric equal to the width of the quilt plus 2 inches for side hems. Generally, 6-inch wide strips will accommodate most rods. If you are using a rod with a larger diameter, increase the width of the strips.

Seam the strips together to get the length needed; press. Fold the strip in half lengthwise, wrong sides together. Stitch the long raw edges together with a 1/4-inch seam allowance. Center the seam on the backside of the sleeve; press. The raw edges of the seam will be concealed when the sleeve is stitched to the back of the quilt. Turn under both of the short raw edges; press and stitch to hem the ends. The final measurement should be about 1/2 inch from the quilt edges.

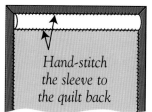

Hand-stitch the sleeve to the quilt back

213

Pin the sleeve to the back of the quilt so the top edge of the sleeve is just below the binding. Hand-stitch the top edge of the sleeve in place, then the bottom edge. Make sure to knot and secure your stitches at each end of the sleeve to make sure it will not pull away from the quilt with use. Slip the rod into the casing. If your wall quilt is not directional, making a sleeve for the bottom edge will allow you to turn your quilt end to end to relieve the stress at the top edge. You could also slip a dowel into the bottom sleeve to help anchor the lower edge of the wall quilt.

Choosing a Quilt Design

Quilting is such an individual process that it is difficult to recommend designs for each quilt. There are hundreds of quilting stencils available at quilt shops. (Templates are used generally for appliqué shapes; stencils are used for marking quilting designs.)

There are a few suggestions that may help you decide how to quilt your project, depending on how much time you would like to spend quilting. Many quilters now use professional long-arm quilting machines or hire someone skilled at running these machines to do the quilting. This, of course, frees up more time to piece.

Quilting Suggestions

Repeat one of the design elements in the quilt as part of the quilting design.

Two or three parallel rows of echo quilting outside an appliqué piece will highlight the shape.

Stipple or meander quilting behind a feather or central motif will make the primary design more prominent.

Look for quilting designs that will cover two or more borders, rather than choosing separate designs for each individual border.

Quilting in the ditch of seams is an effective way to get a project quilted without a great deal of time marking the quilt.

Marking the Quilting Design

When marking the quilt top, use a marking tool that will be visible on the quilt fabric and yet will be easy enough to remove. Always test your marking tool on a scrap of fabric before marking the entire quilt.

Along with a multitude of commercial marking tools available, you may find that very thin slivers of hand soap (Dial, Ivory, etc.) work really well for marking medium to dark color fabrics. The thin lines of soap show up nicely and they are easily removed by simply rubbing gently with a piece of like-colored fabric.

Hints and Helps for Pressing Strip Sets

When sewing strips of fabric together for strip sets, it is important to press the seam allowances nice and flat, usually to the darker fabric. Be careful not to stretch as you press, causing a "rainbow effect." This will affect the accuracy and shape of the pieces cut from the strip set. I like to press on the wrong side first and with the strips perpendicular to the ironing board. Then I flip the piece over and press on the right side to prevent little pleats from forming at the seams. Laying the strip set lengthwise on the ironing board seems to encourage the rainbow effect, as shown in the diagram.

Avoid this rainbow effect

Borders

NOTE: Cut borders to the width called for. Always cut border strips a few inches longer than needed, just to be safe. Diagonally piece the border strips together as needed.

1. With pins, mark the center points along all 4 sides of the quilt. For the top and bottom borders, measure the quilt from left to right through the middle.

2. Measure and mark the border lengths and center points on the strips cut for the borders before sewing them on.

Trim away excess fabric

3. Pin the border strips to the quilt and stitch a 1/4-inch seam. Press the seam allowances toward the border. Trim off excess border lengths.

4. For the side borders, measure your quilt from top to bottom, including the borders just added, to determine the length of the side borders.

5. Measure and mark the side border lengths as you did for the top and bottom borders.

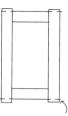

Trim away excess fabric

6. Pin and stitch the side border strips in place. Press and trim the border strips even with the borders just added.

7. If your quilt has multiple borders, measure, mark, and sew additional borders to the quilt in the same manner.

Decorative Stitches

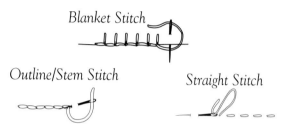

Blanket Stitch

Outline/Stem Stitch

Straight Stitch

Finishing the Quilt

1. Remove the selvages from the backing fabric. Sew the long edges together, and press. Trim the backing and batting so they are 2 inches to 4 inches larger than the quilt top.

2. Mark the quilt top for quilting. Layer the backing, batting, and quilt top. Baste the 3 layers together and quilt.

3. When quilting is complete, remove basting. Hand-baste all 3 layers together a scant 1/4 inch from the edge. This hand-basting keeps the layers from shifting and prevents puckers from forming when adding the binding. Trim excess batting and backing fabric even with the edge of the quilt top. Add the binding as shown below.

Binding and Diagonal Piecing

Diagonal Piecing

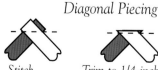

Stitch diagonally

Trim to 1/4-inch seam allowance

Press seam open

1. Diagonally piece the binding strips. Fold the strip in half lengthwise, wrong sides together, and press.

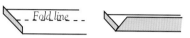

Double-layer Binding

2. Unfold and trim one end at a 45° angle. Turn under the edge 3/8- inch and press. Refold the strip.

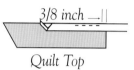

Fold line

3. With raw edges of the binding and quilt top even, stitch with a 3/8-inch seam allowance, starting 2 inches from the angled end.

4. Miter the binding at the corners. As you approach a corner of the quilt, stop sewing 3/8 inch from the corner of the quilt.

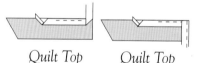

3/8 inch

Quilt Top

5. Clip the threads and remove the quilt from under the presser foot. Flip the binding strip up and away from the quilt, then fold the binding down even with the raw edge of the quilt. Begin sewing at the upper edge. Miter all 4 corners in this manner.

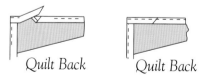

Quilt Top   Quilt Top

6. Trim the end of the binding so it can be tucked inside of the beginning binding about 3/8 inch. Finish stitching the seam.

Quilt Back   Quilt Back

7. Turn the folded edge of the binding over the raw edges and to the back of the quilt so that the stitching line does not show. Hand-sew the binding in place, folding in the mitered corners as you stitch.

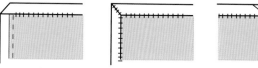

Quilt Back   Quilt Back   Quilt Back

215

For Lynette Jensen, choosing a quilting design

to complement the finished quilt requires as much attention as the construction

of the quilt itself. Three methods of quilting that work well for a variety of quilts

are described below. On the pages that follow, you'll find several examples of

quilting guides that combine to enhance the overall design of the finished quilt.

* OUTLINE QUILTING follows the outline and accentuates the shape of a pieced or appliquéd block by stitching very close to the seam line or as much as 1/4 inch away from the seam line.

* BACKGROUND QUILTING fills large spaces and puts more emphasis on the quilt patterns by making them stand out from the background. Background quilting can be done in straight lines or in a random pattern.

* DESIGN QUILTING is often a decorative accent in its own right. Popular designs include feathers, wreaths, cables, and swags which work well in open spaces such as large corner blocks or borders.

Outline Quilting

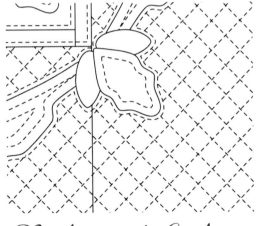

Background Quilting

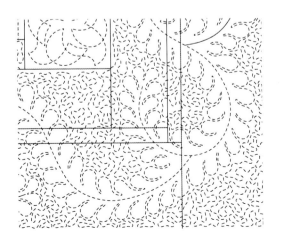

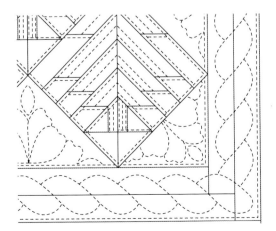

Design Quilting

The QUILTING

Leaf Gathering

A quilting guide to…
Block Party

Stencils used: Thimbleberries® Flutterbug TB35 (3") and Radish Top TB9 (7") *www.quiltingcreations.com*

Block Party

A quilting guide to...
Holly Goose Chase

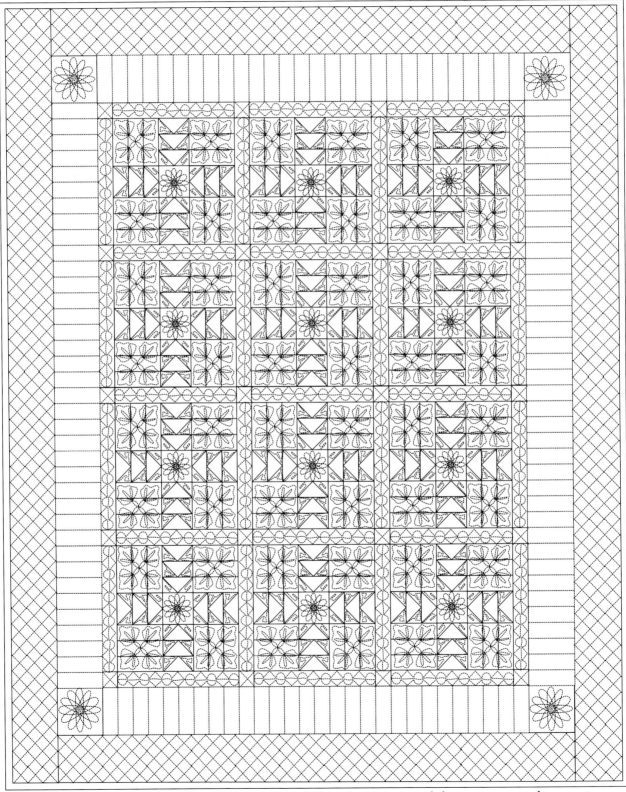

Stencils used: Thimbleberries® Leaf Quartet TB6 (5") and generic spiral design   *www.quiltingcreations.com*

Holly Goose Chase

A quilting guide to...
Hourglass Patches

Stencils used: Thimbleberries® Water Lily TB15 (7"), Mirrored Spring TB41 (8"x6") and Beadwork TB30 (1-1/2") *www.quiltingcreations.com*

Hourglass Patches

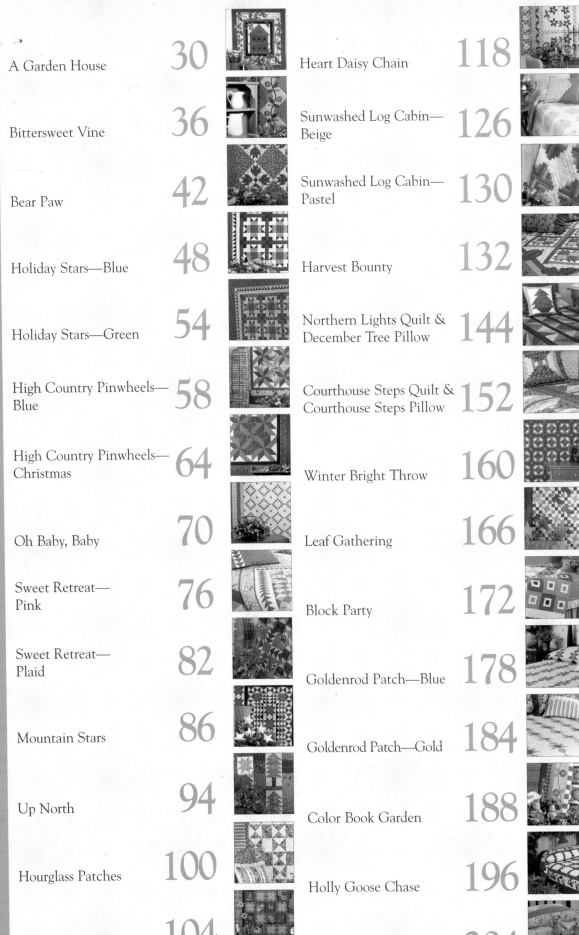

Project INDEX